A **MELVIN DIXON** CRITICAL READER

# A **MELVIN DIXON**
## CRITICAL READER

Edited by Justin A. Joyce and Dwight A. McBride

UNIVERSITY PRESS OF MISSISSIPPI

JACKSON

MARGARET WALKER ALEXANDER SERIES IN AFRICAN AMERICAN STUDIES

www.upress.state.ms.us

The University Press of Mississippi is a member of the Association
of American University Presses.

First Edition 2006

∞

Library of Congress Cataloging-in-Publication Data

Dixon, Melvin, 1950–
    A Melvin Dixon critical reader / edited by Justin A. Joyce and
Dwight A. McBride.— 1st ed.
        p. cm.
    Includes index.
    ISBN 1-57806-866-5 (alk. paper)
    1. American literature—African American authors—History and criticism.
2. African Americans—Intellectual life. 3. African Americans in literature.
I. Joyce, Justin A. II. McBride, Dwight A. III. Title.
    PS153.N5M577 2006
    818'.5409—dc22                                                2005035350

British Library Cataloging-in-Publication Data available

# CONTENTS

# ACKNOWLEDGMENTS

We gratefully acknowledge the following for their kind permission to reprint these essays in this volume:

University of Illinois Press for "Toward a World Black Literature & Community," reprinted from *Chant of Saints: A Gathering of Afro-American Literature, Art, and Scholarship*, eds. Michael S. Harper, Robert B. Stepto, and John Hope Franklin (1979), 175–94.

Modern Language Association of America, MLA Book Publications for "Rivers Remembering Their Source: Comparative Studies in Black Literary History—Langston Hughes, Jacques Roumain, and Négritude," reprinted by permission of the Modern Language Association of America from *Afro-American Literature: The Reconstruction of Instruction*, eds. Dexter Fisher and Robert B. Stepto (1979), 25–43.

Random House, Inc., for "Singing a Deep Song: Language as Evidence in the Novels of Gayl Jones," reprinted from *Black Women Writers (1950–1980): A Critical Evaluation*, ed. Mari Evans (1984), 236–48. © 1983 by Mari Evans. Used by permission of Doubleday, a division of Random House, Inc.

College Language Association and *CLA Journal* for "The Teller as Folk Trickster in Chestnutt's *The Conjure Woman*," reprinted from *CLA Journal* 18 (December 1974): 186–97.

Deanna Dixon and the Melvin Dixon Estate for the following:

"The Black Writer's Use of Memory," originally published in *History and Memory in African-American Culture*, eds. Genevieve Fabre and Robert O'Meally (New York: Oxford University Press, 1994), 18–27.

"Swinging Swords: The Literary Legacy of Slavery," originally published in *The Slave's Narrative: Texts and Contexts*, eds. Henry Louis Gates, Jr., and Charles T. Davis (New York: Oxford University Press, 1985), 298–317.

"Black Theater: The Aesthetics," originally published in *Negro Digest* (July 1969): 41–44.

"Richard Wright: Native Father and His Long Dream (*The Unfinished Quest of Richard Wright*: A Review Essay)," originally published in *Black World* 23 (March 1974): 91–95.

"I'll Be Somewhere Listening for My Name," originally published in *Callaloo* 23 (Winter 2000): 80–83.

Jonathan Silin, Executor of the Estate of Robert Giard, for cover photograph.

Every reasonable effort has been made to trace the copyright holders and to obtain permission for the reprint of copyrighted material. The editors and publishers will gladly receive any information enabling us to rectify any error or omission in subsequent editions.

# INTRODUCTION

*Dixon's Life, Art, and Criticism*

For those familiar with the writing of Melvin Dixon, they know that the experience of an initial encounter with him is on par with that of coming upon one of our nation's most talented writers for the first time. For many, Dixon was our generation's black gay literary treasure, cut off too soon. Not allowed to reach his prime. After co-editing a special issue of the journal *Callaloo* with Jennifer Brody titled "Plum Nelly: New Essays in Black Queer Studies," which was dedicated to the memory of Melvin Dixon and Audre Lorde, Dwight A. McBride began to think that it was important that the world not only know what Dixon accomplished as a fiction writer, but that it also have an opportunity to encounter him as a scholar of African American and Black Diaspora literature and culture. This might allow a generation of readers and scholars to gain a greater appreciation for how Dixon's fiction writing and his critical commentary informed one another in meaningful ways.

The planning for this book project began in earnest after the publication of "Plum Nelly," which McBride co-edited in 2000 while Justin A. Joyce was his research assistant at the University of Illinois at Chicago. As usual in academic life, there was no time. There were already too many obligations and writing projects jockeying for attention. But this simply had to be done because of the many times we have taught Dixon's work, especially *Vanishing Rooms*, and because of the somewhat prophetic nature of the task at hand. Allow us to explain. As we began to put together some thoughts about how to proceed with this introduction, we came across a passage from Dixon's keynote address to the queer writers' conference, OutWrite 1992, in Boston when he summarized specifically what he saw as the future of gay and lesbian publishing. We might receive those same words today as a blueprint for the larger preservation and extension of black queer studies. Dixon wrote:

> First, reaffirm the importance of cultural diversity in our community. Second, preserve our literary heritage by posthumous publications and reprints, and third, establish grants and fellowships to ensure that our literary history is written and passed on to others. I don't think these comments are bleak, but they should remind us of one thing: We alone are responsible for the preservation and future of our literature.
>
> If we don't buy our books, they won't get published. If we don't talk about our books, they won't get reviewed. If we don't write our books, they won't get written.[1]

These prophetic and poignant words spoken by Dixon in 1992, the very same year that he died of an AIDS-related illness, are as true today as ever. They make us proud to be a part of a project that would see Dixon's words—his powerful and still cogent words— back in print for another generation of readers who so desperately need his voice. Dixon's is an artistic talent that set the bar of literary achievement in black queer fiction very high, indeed. In fact, had he not died so young, we do not think that we overstate the case to say that Dixon was well on his way to being this generation's James Baldwin.

Melvin Winfred Dixon was born May 29, 1950, in Stamford, Connecticut, to Handy and Jessie Dixon. He attended college at Wesleyan University where he received his B.A. with high honors in 1971. He then pursued his graduate studies at Brown University where he received his master's degree in 1973 and his Ph.D. in 1975 in American Civilization. His dissertation at Brown was entitled "Historical Vision and Personal Witness in American Slave Literature," wherein he discussed "the slave's life experience as it relates to the formation of belief patterns within the slave community." Analyses of the slave songs and of slave narratives were central to his project. After completing his doctoral studies, Dixon accepted an appointment at Wesleyan University as assistant professor of English where he served from 1976 to 1980. In 1980 he accepted an appointment to the faculty of Queens College of the City University of New York as associate professor. In 1986 he was promoted to full professor at Queens College. Dixon died on October 26, 1992, at age forty-two of complications from the AIDS virus.

Dixon distinguished himself in several literary genres. He was a poet, novelist, literary critic, and translator. He published a collection of poems in 1983 entitled *Change of Territory: Poems*, and in part through the efforts of fellow-poet and literary critic Elizabeth Alexander, *Love's Instruments* was posthumously published in 1995. *Change of Territory*—in many ways a poetic rendering of the critical concerns that Dixon elaborates in *Ride Out the Wilderness: Geography and Identity in Afro-American Literature* (1987)—represents the fusing of the critical and artistic talents that Dixon's work illustrates so well. Literary critic Hermine D. Pinson observes about *Change of Territory* that it "charts decisive moments in the poet/protagonist's journey from childhood to manhood and the genealogical tributaries that shape and inform his voice. Filling out the poet's 'song' is a panoply of voices that range from the individual: enslaved African forefather, grandmother, mother, and father, to the collective: Teddy Wilson, James P. Johnson, Romare Bearden, and Ralph Ellison, artists who are a part of the history of the black expressive tradition."² If, as Pinson observes, *Change of Territory* chronicles the individual's response over time and space to the persistent externally imposed forces of race, sexuality, and class, it would appear that part of that history is also the marginalizing of gay sexuality. If that marginalization is deliberate, as Pinson believes it is, Dixon actually addresses the intersection of race and gay sexuality by framing the text with these issues. After all, as she rightly observes, "the speaker embarks from home a black gay male, and returns home a black gay male." Here, again, we witness the critical mind powerfully at work through artistic expression. What *Change of Territory* may not yield in direct address of black gay sexuality is more than made up for in Dixon's posthumously published poetry collection, *Love's Instruments*.

In *Love's Instruments*, Dixon dramatizes his experience of living with AIDS. According to Carla Williams, one of the poems in the collection, "Aunt Ida Pieces a Quilt," "explains how a dead man's garments are gathered to be included in his grandmother's contribution to the AIDS Memorial Quilt. This nostalgic description of the traditional black women's craft, juxtaposed with the modern reality of loss, lies at the heart of Dixon's work."³ And, indeed, it does. We see this tradition/modern reality connection at work in many of the pieces in the volume. "Turning Forty in the 90's" provides a haunting portrait of loss and love by addressing how a couple in their forties must face their premature mortality:

> *We promised to grow old together, our dream*
> *since years ago when we began*
> *to celebrate our common tenderness*
> *and touch. So here we are:*

*Dry, ashy skin, falling hair, losing breath*
*at the top of the stairs, forgetting things.*
*Vials of Septra and AZT line the bedroom dresser*
*like a boy's toy army poised for attack—*
*your red, my blue, and the casualties are real.*

Another poem in the volume, "One by One," speaks to the poet's urgency to document and leave a written record of his life and work before it is too late. In the spirit of a consumption-laden John Keats who wrote "When I have fears that I may cease to be . . . ," Dixon in his bout with AIDS also worries about running out of time:

*The children in the life:*
*Another telephone call. Another man gone.*
*How many pages are left in my diary?*
*Do I have enough pencils? Enough ink?*
*I count on my fingers and toes the past kisses,*
*the incubating years, the months ahead.*

The poem's refrain, "many thousands gone," is a reference to the Negro spiritual "No More Auction Block for Me" that insists on the connectedness of Dixon's black gay identity with that of the larger African American community. Here, as elsewhere in the collection, Dixon does not allow his sexuality to separate him from black culture (signaled here by reference to the Negro spiritual) or from the black community. Indeed, as Williams suggests, "Dixon embraced his community and demanded that his community embrace him in return."

Along with his poetry, he was the author of another novel in addition to his 1991 *Vanishing Rooms*, which was titled *Trouble the Water* (1989). His major work of literary criticism was *Ride Out the Wilderness: Geography and Identity in Afro-American Literature* (1987).

And his best-known works of translation were French literary critic Genevieve Fabre's *Drumbeats, Masks, and Metaphor: Contemporary Afro-American Theatre* (1983) and *The Collected Poems of Léopold Sédar Senghor* (1991). In addition to serving as a contributing and advisory editor to *Callaloo: A Journal of African-American and African Arts and Letters*, Dixon also published numerous essays and works of short fiction in a variety of venues.

*Ride Out the Wilderness* was Dixon's debut critical book, and if we take seriously his comments in an interview with Jerome de Romanet in the pages of *Callaloo*, he thought of it as his last book of criticism. This was not because of his illness, but rather because of his growing disenchantment with the state of critical theory in the academy:

> I don't think I would ever do another book of criticism. . . . I think what really did it was when people became so theoretical, and literary theory became so, you know, it was like a fire storm, and it was so boring to me, where scholars felt they had to make some connection between Derrida and Faulkner, and all the discussions began with an assessment of critical theory, and everyone had to become theoretical. And it was such an easy way of getting out of the responsibility of reading literature and talking about technique. So, I guess that the straw that broke the camel's back for me was the fact that literary theorists were building a reputation by engaging in a dialogue with other theorists, and forgetting all about the fact that there is a text somewhere. So, I became more and more disillusioned with the way in which academic work was progressing, and I thought that the academic work, you know, academics were just less interesting for me, and it wasn't challenging . . .[4]

In many ways these comments provide a context for what *Ride Out the Wilderness* achieves as a work of criticism. Literary critic

Cheryl A. Wall, in a review of Dixon's book, writes that he largely "banishes theory from his text."[5] While Wall is right that Dixon does not employ the language of theorists most readily associated with post-structuralist theory, which was in critical vogue when *Ride Out the Wilderness* was published, this does not mean that he had no ideas about the nature of theory as it should be applied to African American texts. Indeed, in an age when the recognized leaders of the field of African American literary studies had intensified their efforts to demonstrate the utility of post-structuralist theory to examinations of African American literary texts (Spillers, "Mama's Baby, Papa's Maybe"—1987; Henderson, "Speaking in Tongues"—1989; Baker, "Belief, Theory, and Blues"—1986; Gates, *The Signifying Monkey*—1988), Dixon seems to hold out for the possibility that aesthetic criticism still has much to teach us about African American literature:

> I find myself alone in a sense, because people are more interested today in ideas and theory rather than the aesthetic experience of reading a good poem, or writing, or talking about a good poem. No one even talks about what makes this poem pleasurable, aesthetically. No one talks about that: you have to talk about the issue of gender, the issues of stuff, stuff, stuff. . . . You never talk about how the poem achieves its beauty as a poem. I'm not trying to justify my deliberate choice by blaming the theorists, but what I'm saying is that I have found writing criticism and scholarship far less satisfying, and far less meaningful to me than writing fiction and poetry, even if it's bad fiction and poetry. There's something more challenging—and it's the hardest thing to do—than sit around and repeat what Derrida said, or Foucault said. (de Romanet/Dixon 85)

It is not that Dixon is anti-theory; he is opposed to theory that is not based in, centered on, and concerned with the primacy of the text and its aesthetics. It is an artist/critic's position. Likely, Dixon expresses here a common concern that African American creative writers at the time had about the direction of African American literary criticism. Post-structuralist theory's advent in the African American literary academy occasioned a "firestorm" of sorts among black critics that is well documented (the famed *New Literary History* Debate between Joyce A. Joyce, Henry Louis Gates, Jr., and Houston A. Baker, Jr., is a most notable example of this); and the battle lines were drawn quite dramatically. Quite as it's kept, the schisms that persist to this day in the African American literary academy between writers and critics, between traditional critics and theorists, can be understood as manifestations of this particular history.

*Ride Out the Wilderness*, produced as it was at this critical juncture in African American letters, is a text that tries to articulate a theory of African American literature and identity by looking first and foremost to African American writing for its cues. In the book, Dixon self-avowedly sets out to "examine the ways in which Afro-American writers, often considered homeless, alienated from mainstream culture, and segregated in negative environments, have used language to create alternative landscapes where black culture and identity can flourish apart from any marginal, prescribed 'place'" (2). As Wall reminds us,

> If the blues are one mother lode of Afro-American verbal art, the spirituals are another, though one which critics infrequently mine. Melvin Dixon's *Ride Out the Wilderness* should change that. The study's organizing metaphors—the wilderness, the underground, and the mountaintop—are drawn from the slave songs and traced through a broad selection of texts. These range from *Cane* to *Corregidora*, *Banana Bottom* to *Just above My Head*. In all, Dixon places the work of ten twentieth-century writers in fruitful intertextual relation (682).

It is precisely this kind of critical project that interests Dixon the artist as well. In a comment about *Ride Out the Wilderness*, Dixon states: "I don't begin with any theoretical formulation at all, but I try to let the writers tell me what the larger issues are . . . and they do!" He is interested in the tropes, the language, and the aesthetics that the culture gives to the writer/artist. He queries the manner in which they are put to use, revised, and extended by artists in the tradition, and examined by the critics of the tradition. For Dixon the black literary tradition is rich, broad, and as cosmopolitan as he himself was:

> But what I think is absolutely crucial—I don't know how to emphasize this more strongly—what I learned living in France and living in West Africa is that it is absolutely crucial for people of color to see themselves globally, rather than domestically. There is no way in the world that you can tell me that the African-American experience is a minority experience, now. But how many of us grow up thinking that we are minorities? And even that one term restricts your entire perspective on this: suddenly, your world is diminished to the way in which white Americans think about you; and how dare you define yourself solely through the prejudices and the narrowness of one ethnic group? So, I tell people all the time that minority is not even in my vocabulary anymore, because in the world, people of color aren't in the minority! (de Romanet/Dixon 101)

While in *A Melvin Dixon Critical Reader* we reprint for the ready access of scholars, readers, and writers Dixon's published essays, we also recognize the extent to which Dixon the scholar informed Dixon the fiction writer and vice-versa. The form of his fiction was as challenging and invigorating as any scholarly monograph, and at the same time as beautiful as a well-wrought poem. So, by way of introducing Dixon's critical voice, we tarry first in the world of his fiction—particularly *Vanishing Rooms*—to observe a formidable intellect at work that is equally at home in the formal or the aesthetic milieu.

*Vanishing Rooms* is principally set in 1975 New York City with flash-backs referring to earlier periods in the characters' lives that both inform much of who they are and give the reader clues as to where their perceptions of their world come from. The novel's ensemble cast includes: Metro, a murdered, Southern, white journalist who lived in Greenwich Village with his lover Jesse until Jesse falls victim to the homophobic violence that so brutally and needlessly ends his life; Jesse, a black, college-educated dancer left to mourn and recon-struct the death of his lover and the meaning of the events of their life together; Ruella, a black, heterosexual female dancer who befriends and falls in love with Jesse and who also has her own family history with which she must come to terms; and Lonny, a sexually repressed, working-class, Italian youth who was among the company of those who raped and murdered Metro. Of these characters, only Metro is not a narrator. The other three each, in turn, narrate the entirety of the novel's action in prose that is at turns hauntingly visceral and beautiful. The question remains, however, as to why Dixon, who published *Vanishing Rooms* in 1991, chose 1975 (incidentally the same year he finished his Ph.D. at Brown) as the setting for his novel. As a way of coming to some conclusions about what might prompt Dixon to set his story some fifteen years before its publication date, let us recall what the popular American landscape looked like in 1975. After all, is there anything in the novel that requires this specific period location? Or could it just as easily have taken place in Dixon's present of the early 1990s?

The year 1975 was a significant year in many respects in American history. The nation was coming out of the very important—even if tumultuous, strife-ridden, and bloody—period of the 1960s. This included several very high-profile assassinations, the peak of the Civil Rights Movement, the Bay of Pigs, the Cuban missile crisis, and the final withdrawal of American troops from Vietnam. On April 30, 1975, the last Americans, ten Marines from the embassy, departed Saigon. This concluded the United States' presence in Vietnam, clearing the way for the North Vietnamese to claim victory. It is important to recall that the Vietnam War was itself quite tied with how African Americans perceived their future on the national agenda.

President Lyndon Johnson's War Against Poverty included a Community Action Plan (CAP) that allowed local citizens to organize using federal funds from the Office of Economic Opportunity. Many such funds went into teaching the poor how to take action against slumlords and ineffective city bureaucrats, which resulted in alienating the mayors of cities like Los Angeles and Chicago. Senator Daniel Patrick Moynihan of New York, who in 1965 was an assistant secretary of labor in the Johnson administration, wrote a report entitled "The Negro Family: The Case for National Action." The now infamous report took a "blame the victim" stance on the problem of the black family and black poverty, which did not sit well with a black public who perceived the government's spending on the Vietnam War as a needless drain on funds that could otherwise be used to forward their agenda on domestic programs like the Job Corps and Head Start. Congress disagreed, however, and voted to continue U.S. involvement in Vietnam. Going into 1968, President Johnson had effectively alienated black Americans, a major source of traditional support for the Democratic Party, who thought the United States should withdraw from its expensive campaign in Vietnam.

Despite a degree of difficulty and some resistance, by 1975 many Americans were moving the country in a decidedly more humane direction. The year 1975 saw the passage of the Age Discrimination Act whose purpose was to prohibit discrimination on the basis of age in programs or activities receiving federal financial assistance. The abuse of the elderly that the Act was intended to remedy also saw expression that same year in a kind of hyperbolic satire presented in Paul Bartel's film *Death Race 2000*. In the film, participants in this bloody transcontinental race win points by running over pedestrians. The main character, Frankenstein, kills several invalids (anyone over age seventy is worth one hundred points, the highest awarded) who have been put in the middle of the road for "Euthanasia Day" at the hospital. In 1975 Americans were also beginning to take more stock of disabilities that we consider commonplace today. For example, the Dyslexia Research Institute, from its inception in 1975, had as its goal to change the perception of learning differences, specifically in the area of dyslexia and attention deficit disorders (ADD). In addition, issues of sexual diversity were increasingly coming to the fore publicly. The year 1975 saw the release of a now camp cult classic, *The Rocky Horror Picture Show*, just on the heels of the 1973 launch of *Interview*, a magazine centered upon Andy Warhol's fascination with the cult of celebrity, and the 1974 release of Paul Morrissey and Warhol's films *Frankenstein* and *Dracula*.

In an even more popular vein, *One Flew over The Cuckoo's Nest* won the Academy Award for Best Picture in 1975. The pop music charts in 1975 were topped by the following ten hits:

1. *Love Will Keep Us Together*, Captain & Tennille (A&M)
2. *Philadelphia Freedom*, Elton John (MCA)
3. *Rhinestone Cowboy*, Glen Campbell (Capitol)
4. *My Eyes Adored You*, Frankie Valli (Private Stock)
5. *That's the Way I Like It*, KC & The Sunshine Band (T.K.)
6. *Shining Star*, Earth, Wind & Fire (Columbia)
7. *Fame*, David Bowie (RCA)
8. *Laughter in the Rain*, Neil Sedaka (MCA)

9. *One of These Nights*, Eagles (Asylum)
10. *Thank God I'm a Country Boy*, John Denver (RCA)

The New York-centered television shows *Saturday Night Live* and *Barney Miller* both premiered in 1975. Also in 1975, two young entrepreneurs in Albuquerque, New Mexico, Bill Gates and Paul Allen, launched the BASIC programming language for the ALTAIR 8800, the first product for the then fledgling Microsoft Corporation. This same year witnessed the invention of the laser printer and the push-through tab on the drink can. This was preceded by the invention of the all-important post-it note in 1974.

So why 1975? First of all biographically, it is important to note that Dixon himself says that he wrote the first page of *Vanishing Rooms* in France in 1979 (de Romanet/Dixon 88). So the fact that the book was conceived in that period, would help explain the choice to set it in 1975. This period of 1975 also coincided with Dixon's time as a graduate student. This was a time in which he traveled a great deal and perhaps was most self-consciously aware of the cultural milieu in which he wrote. We are also convinced that 1975 was a time when the public terms in which sexual identity questions were being discussed were still under construction to a greater degree than they were in the late eighties and early nineties. And this is not even to mention the fact that this latter period was further complicated by the height of the AIDS epidemic, a topic Dixon may have wished to avoid by choosing to set *Vanishing Rooms* in 1975 so that the AIDS epidemic would not overshadow the other very important problems central to this novel: the nature of interracial intimacy, relationships between gay men and heterosexual women, the violent manifestations of homophobia, and the relationship between love and desire to name but a few. Finally, as we stated before, the mid-seventies was a time when the nation was exploring what it meant to realize the more humane America that had been brought about as a result of the hard-fought battles of the sixties. This provides a most appropriate backdrop to the interconnected stories of our ensemble cast of characters who each in turn give us the truth that is *Vanishing Rooms*.

While Dixon's first novel, *Trouble the Water*, received a great deal of mainstream critical attention,[6] it is *Vanishing Rooms* that seems to be leading in the area of scholarly commentary. Some critics have suggested that *Vanishing Rooms* is a novel in which categories like "truth" are highly "contested."[7] We submit that Dixon is not inviting us toward an understanding of the nature of truth as "contested" as much as he is pointing out the inherent complexity of truth and of truth-telling. Dixon urges us toward an understanding of truth that is more like the four parts of his novel. If we take his decision to have three different narrators give their unique perspectives on a common event in each part of the novel, we begin to see Dixon's understanding of truth come into clearer focus. For Dixon, the *event* of Metro's brutal death is not the same as the *truth* of the event. Countless events that occur in our world daily go unremarked. It is when events are deemed "significant," or when they are called upon to be meaningful, that truth becomes involved. Events can have a variety of different meanings, or they may not mean anything at all. When we need for them to mean, is when the matter of truth enters the picture.

For Dixon, the event is like the city of New York itself (where *Vanishing Rooms* is set). Its spatial and temporal existence is self-evident. But the truth of the city, like the truth of the event of Metro's death, varies with the four seasons and with the three narrators. The truth of the event unfolds with the passage of time, which involves experience, narrative, and memory. So, if you experience the city in the spring it is the same as, but clearly also different from, experiencing the city in the winter. Therefore, truth is not so much contested for

Dixon as it is complicated. The versions of it are not "competing," so much as they are "complementing" and "completing" one another.

Dixon also points out the unusual circumstance of his reader. Similar to the situation of a courtroom, wherein witnesses are called upon and interrogated in order to elicit their truth of the event there in question, the reader—like the judge and jury—gets to hear all of the complementing and completing truths. But it is, perhaps, only in the world of narrative fiction (and not even in the courtroom) that one can hear not only the testimony suitable for public consumption, but also hear it interwoven with those aspects of the story unavailable to us otherwise. In the world of fiction, we get to hear the private, internal testimony. Done well, as in the case of Dixon's story, the narrative both intensifies and then satisfies the reader's desire for that certain, internal, private something so very difficult to come by elsewhere in our lives.

Textually, *Vanishing Rooms*, like a handful of novels before it that have used multiple narration, is a virtuoso performance which both celebrates and exploits the fundamental dishonesty of linear narrative storytelling. Dixon's novel achieves in print what the films *Short Cuts* (1993); *Pulp Fiction* (1994); *Run, Lola, Run* (1998); and *Magnolia* (1999) accomplished cinematically. By getting inside a narrating character and seeing the world created in the novel from his or her perspective, we are given something more than the normal opportunity in linear, singular narration. In addition to seeing what characters in novels mean from the typical perspective of the main character, multiple perspectives are provided by an ensemble of narrators. In linear narrative fiction of the kind that Dixon resists writing in *Vanishing Rooms*, minor characters are flat and achieve meaning primarily by how they figure into the larger narrative perspective of the main character. The very language of "main" and "minor" characters and of "plot" and "sub-plots" are used to describe such linear fictions. Again, like the ensemble casts of the movies just mentioned, we would be hard pressed to say who the "main character" is in *Vanishing Rooms*. The event itself becomes the main character, and the narrative product the very complicated truth of its telling. This is, at least in part, what makes *Vanishing Rooms* such an exciting and gripping novel which ". . . allows us to question reality without making the question of reality the big intellectual issue. It becomes the issue when we see how so much of our personalities are informed by how we see the world" (de Romanet/Dixon 88). At once an incredible achievement as a work of fiction, *Vanishing Rooms* is also a work that demands its readers to think differently about the very nature of narrative and truth. This is one small example of why we get the most from reading Dixon by taking him seriously as both artist and critic. As poet and essayist Elizabeth Alexander reminds us about Dixon: "He was a writer and a scholar who refused to draw hard and fast distinctions between the activities of the sides of the brain. He called himself a 'person of letters' whose religion was writing, whatever form it took."[8]

It is with enormous pleasure that we present for the first time Melvin Dixon's eight published critical essays in a single volume. The scholarly contributions represented by these pieces will be of service to scholars, readers, and writers interested in black Diaspora studies, African American literary criticism and theory, francophone literature scholars, folklorists, and so much more for years to come. The breadth represented in these essays is equaled only by Dixon's intense commitment to exploring the varieties of African American and black gay experiences in his fiction and poetry. Dixon is a writer for our times. We trust this book will help us to remember him.

In "Toward a World Black Literature & Community," Dixon explores the influence and thematic concerns of writers of the African Diaspora, specifically concentrating on themes of racial community, which Dixon theorizes has produced a literature that "define[s] man in relation to his particular ethnic, regional, and national identity, and examine[s] the universal conflict between the individual and society." Dixon here presents a critique of the Harlem Renaissance, the African Négritude movement, and the Haitian and Caribbean Indigenist movements by offering a detailed analysis of three novels, which Dixon identifies as respectively representative of each of these major movements: Claude McKay's *Banjo*, Rene Maran's *Batouala*, and Jacques Roumain's *Masters of the Dew*.

"Rivers Remembering Their Source: Comparative Studies in Black Literary History—Langston Hughes, Jacques Roumain, and Négritude" continues Dixon's diasporic interests. His opening claim that the "single most resounding literary achievement of international scale in the twentieth century has been the development of Négritude, the celebration of black consciousness through literature," rings out almost as loudly as the summary call to action with which he ends this piece. Yet, the clarity and precision with which Dixon leads us through his argument are what stand out most. As a means of establishing parallels, Dixon points us to Richard Wright's comment that black writers—whether of the Harlem Renaissance, the Haitian Indigenist movement, or any writer or movement throughout the African Diaspora (regardless of geographical, temporal, or national delineations)—all face the same challenge. They must confront the challenge to create "a language that is faithful to the experience of blacks in the New World, a language that expresses the acculturation of traditional African and European forms and the dynamic transformation and reinvention of the self that results." For Dixon, this challenge is met through language that encompasses the American experience of blending and borrowing, a language "that creates literature from the historical experience of the language and the peculiar cultural syncretism from which it was born." As examples, Dixon leads us through readings of poetry by José Zacarias Tallet, Langston Hughes, and Jacques Roumain, specifically concentrating on the linguistic similarities in the poetry of Roumain and Hughes in order to substantiate his claims of cross-fertilization and intertextuality among works of New World black literature.

Finally, Dixon briefly discusses Edward Brathwaite's identification and distinction of four types of New World literatures that comment on the African presence, stressing that the most important and most readily applicable to this piece is the "literature of African expression." With its emphasis on folk material and the translation of folk into literary experiment, this "literature of African expression" allows for not only a reinvention of the individual self, but also for a merging of "traditional African oral heritage with the most useful European vocabulary." Thus, it creates a unique language and culture that bonds all writers throughout the Diaspora, despite national or generic delineations.

Perhaps one of Dixon's most often cited and widely read essays, "The Black Writer's Use of Memory," explores the importance of geography, memory, and the construction of African American culture in African American literature. He begins with a short discussion of Pierre Nora's views on the differences between history and memory—namely that Nora understands history as static and memory as dynamic—and then goes on to stress the significance of "*lieux de mémoire*" (i.e., the sites of memory) as markers for a construction and reinvention of cultural identity in African American literature. Dixon briefly discusses prose by Ralph Ellison, Ernest Gaines, and Toni Morrison. This piece also contains a slightly longer discussion of a number of poems by various authors, including Robert Hayden, Countee Cullen, Langston Hughes, Léopold Senghor, Derek Walcott, and Audre Lorde. Finally, Dixon briefly discusses his own poetry and fiction, touching on the significance of history and memory in his poetry collection, *Change of Territory*, and his novel, *Trouble the Water*.

"Swinging Swords: The Literary Legacy of Slavery" examines the importance of slave narratives, Negro spirituals, and oral traditions to African American literature. Dixon characterizes these forms as having what he calls a "seminal" importance to the African American literary tradition. As primary modes of expression from within the slave community, these modes represented a unique voice through the combined embodiment of the slave's uniquely syncretic religion, a critique of the plantation system, a search for freedom and identity, and the presentation of a "heroic fugitive character unlike any other in American literature." There is a discussion here of the origin and importance of the slave's particular religious system and the significance of conversion within the community, which Dixon argues has produced a literature of "struggle and fulfillment."

Dixon also traces a number of recurring images and metaphors and identifies a series of steps or transition points that are found in a majority of slave narratives. First, there is a recognition of slave identity. This is usually followed by a resolve to remedy the situation of racial oppression represented by that identity. Following these markers, there is an impulse for freedom that coincides with changes in the slave's character. These changes lead to a pivotal moment of decision or action, often in response to an episode of especially cruel treatment. The slave's isolation during flight is a period marked by meditation and communion with God (often in the wilderness) and produces a unique moral code suited to the justification of acts that help to secure the slaves' successful escape. Finally, there is a moment of symbolic death and rebirth that marks the crucial transformation between slavery and freedom. Closely aligned with the religious doctrine of struggle and freedom—in no small part derived from the biblical stories of the Children of Israel—this rebirth is often seen as the chief component or goal of these narratives and the lives they portray.

"Black Theater: The Aesthetics" calls for the realization of black aesthetics separate from Western dramatic traditions. Asserting that "the community as a collective society is the center of black aesthetics," Dixon calls for a black aesthetics stemming from within the black community that represents the particular speech, movement, and psychological crisis of a black existence in white America. This essay clearly draws upon some of the conclusions he reaches in *Ride Out the Wilderness* that we discussed earlier.

"Singing a Deep Song: Language as Evidence in the Novels of Gayl Jones" comments on the work of Gayl Jones and her use of black speech as an aesthetic device through which she presents character and theme. Dixon aligns Jones's use of black speech with that of Alice Walker, Toni Morrison, Sherley Ann Williams, Toni Cade Bambara and others who understand black speech as a type of inventive manipulation of language and storytelling, rather than as a representation of dialect. Dixon identifies this transformation of language ("ritualized dialogue") as a distinctive feature of Jones's style which allows her to examine the capacity of language to present character and theme while questioning the ability of this language to facilitate the reconciliation that Dixon fingers as the goal of Jones's characters. Specifically, Dixon presents an exploration of two of Jones's novels, *Corregidora*, and *Eva's Man*. Similar in the ways they present language and idiomatic exchanges, both centered on reconciliation from abusive relationships between men and women, *Corregidora* and *Eva's Man* are seen by Dixon as companion texts that deal with one woman's rise and another's fall.

"The Teller as Folk Trickster in Chestnutt's *The Conjure Woman*" is Dixon's critique of Charles Chesnutt's first novel. Here Dixon examines in depth the complexity of Chesnutt's characters and their relation to the traditional folk trickster. Dixon makes a connection between the character of Julius (the teller of the series of seven folktales that comprise the novel) and Chesnutt himself. Dixon claims that Julius's rhetorical trickery not only unifies the independent stories, but also mirrors Chesnutt's strategic creation of multiple levels of tale-telling and reception, which allowed Chestnutt to present his views to a predominately white audience when the stories were first published in the *Atlantic Monthly* in 1899. Dixon offers an analysis of how each of the tales serves Julius's ulterior motives of material, psychological, or sexual gain from his employer, John, and how the subtle, ironic subterfuge involved in these tales relates to Chesnutt's goal of liberating black representations in fiction from the damaging stereotypes of the Old South and antebellum literature.

In "Richard Wright: Native Father and His Long Dream (*The Unfinished Quest of Richard Wright*: A Review Essay)," Dixon reviews Michel Fabre's biography of Richard Wright, *The Unfinished Quest of Richard Wright*. Dixon examines the scope of this challenging probe into an important life, since Fabre considers Richard Wright's life and work not simply from a literary critical point of view, but with an interest in Wright's political struggles and their historical implications. According to Dixon, Fabre presents Wright's life as that of "a man adapting and growing to realize an ultimate human and artistic expression . . . provid[ing] a framework for political and literary commitment to the international struggle of race and revolution."

It seems only fitting that this book conclude with some of Dixon's most poignant and prophetic words that were spoken in the months leading up to his last days, and that provided much of the inspiration for this volume. "I'll Be Somewhere Listening for My Name" is the speech he delivered at the queer writers' conference, OutWrite 1992, in Boston. In it, he not only eloquently describes the importance and the perils of gay writing (and even more specifically of black gay writing), but he also charges each of us "by the possibility of [our] good health, by the broadness of [our] vision, to remember" those who have fallen. We are to bear witness with our imaginations, our craft, and our pens. Poet and critic Elizabeth Alexander wrote of this speech saying that "it stands as one of the most important essays written about writing in the age of AIDS, and it offers an example of Dixon's prose eloquence, as well as his fierce intellectual and political commitment to the many issues raised by the disease's rampage through our society."[9] Her description of his words is not only apt, but incredibly true. And this speech, along with Dixon's fiction, position him as one of the true pioneers who not only studied that important intersection where race and sexuality meet, but who first helped us to realize that they have always been intertwined.

—Justin A. Joyce
—Dwight A. McBride

## Notes

1. Melvin Dixon, "I'll Be Somewhere Listening for My Name," *Callaloo*, a special issue, eds. Dwight A. McBride and Jennifer DeVere Brody, "Plum Nelly: New Essays in Black Queer Studies," 23.1 (Winter 2000): 82–83.

2. Hermine D. Pinson, "Geography and Identity in Melvin Dixon's *Change of Territory*," *MELUS*, 21:1 (Spring 1996): 97–111.

3. Carla Williams, "Dixon, Melvin," *GLBTQ: An Encyclopedia of Gay, Lesbian, Bisexual, Transgender, & Queer Culture*: www.glbtq.com.

4. Jerome de Romanet, "A Conversation with Melvin Dixon," (an interview) *Callaloo*, a special issue, eds. Dwight A. McBride and Jennifer DeVere Brody, "Plum Nelly: New Essays in Black Queer Studies," 23.1 (Winter 2000): 84.

5. Cheryl A. Wall, review of *Ride Out the Wilderness*, by Melvin Dixon, *American Literature* 60.4 (1988): 682.

6. It was reviewed by many mainstream venues including the *New York Times* and the *Los Angeles Times*.

7. Vivian May, "Reading Melvin Dixon's *Vanishing Rooms*: Experiencing 'the ordinary rope that can change in a second to a lyncher's noose or a rescue line,'" *Callaloo*, a special issue, eds. Dwight A. McBride and Jennifer DeVere Brody, "Plum Nelly: New Essays in Black Queer Studies," 23.1 (Winter 2000): 366.

8. Elizabeth Alexander, introduction, *Love's Instruments*, by Melvin Dixon (Chicago: Tia Chucha Press, 1995), 6.

9. Ibid., 6.

Part I

# WRITING
## **BLACK DIASPORA**
## **THEORY**

# TOWARD A WORLD BLACK
# LITERATURE & COMMUNITY

Writers of the African diaspora continually explore the idea of racial community for theme, imagery, and heroic characterization. Their works, brought to international attention through the French and English language, define man in relation to his particular ethnic, regional, and national identity, and examine the universal conflict between the individual and society. Through the literature of the Harlem Renaissance, the Negritude movement in Africa, the Indigenist movement in Haiti and throughout the Caribbean, modern black writers have identified the broad frontiers of human need and racial progress. Their themes assess the role of the artist within society and the contribution of black peoples to world culture. This thematic concern rejects provincial colonial mentality and expands the goals and dimensions of black life. The quest for community expressed in these New Negro movements presents a point of cultural contact and comparison in the literature and contemporary issues which shaped world black writing during the past fifty years.

In the United States, southern blacks migrated north hoping to share in America's new industrial growth, national identity, and the international success of Allied victory in World War I. North American blacks helped to forge one of the most energetic periods in their cultural history. The Harlem Renaissance generated new racial awareness and encomium as defenses against political disfranchisement, lynchings, and early Jim Crow legislation.

Almost simultaneously, Caribbean populations, particularly in Haiti, suffered similar discrimination under American occupation which began in 1915. Haitian intellectuals, notably Emile Roumer, Jean Price-Mars, Jacques Roumain, Daniel Heurtelou, found a new strength in their identity as black Haitians face to face with a common white intruder. Through their patriotism and spirit of resistance, they became interested in folklore and native traditions, "studied passionately the customs, beliefs, popular tales, and discovered them intact and living well among the Haitian peasants."[1] In 1927 these writers founded *La Revue Indigène*. Of the founders, it was Jacques Roumain who became friends with Langston Hughes and studied at Columbia University in 1932. For years thereafter, even when the review ceased publication, Roumain was to play a "capital role as liaison between the Afro-American renaissance and the indigenist movement."[2]

The Harlem Renaissance was brought to a close by the Depression in 1930. But that year in Paris, a Dr. Sajons of Haiti and sisters Andrée and Paulette Nardal of Martinique founded *La Revue du Monde Noir*, which diffused the ideas of the Renaissance and the Indigenist movement to the black French-speaking world. Paulette Nardal, a student of English, translated many Renaissance poets for the magazine, and, encouraged by René Maran, began translating Alain Locke's *New Negro* into French. Traveling writers offered other means of mutual contact. In the salon of the Nardal sisters, black American writers "met with those who went on to found the Négritude movement."[3] Maran himself became a close friend of Alain Locke and opened his Paris home to Countee Cullen, Claude McKay, James Weldon Johnson, Langston Hughes, and others.

*La Revue du Monde Noir* ceased publication after six issues. Then in 1932 Martiniquan students began *Légitime Défense*, which exposed

West Indian middle-class assimilation, its corruption and prejudice, its "treason towards its own race." With one stroke the West Indian literary tradition, built upon conscious imitation of European writers, was discarded. The tiny brochure caused an enormous sensation and was prohibited almost immediately. Two years later *L'Etudiant Noir* was started by other university students grouped around Léopold Senghor of Senegal, Aimé Césaire of Martinique, and Léon Damas of French Guyana. The magazine attacked cultural assimilation and voiced the grievances of many blacks. The writers rejected France, indeed all of Europe, as a cultural model and encouraged black intellectuals to examine native cultures as well as the impact of the African presence throughout the world.

By 1935 black writers on all three continents were claiming their legitimate defense against cultural exclusion and isolation. They expressed the shared assumptions of racial progress which made ethnic and regional groups cohesive. They changed the course of modern literature by demanding that the African voice be heard. In the span of twenty-five years, 1920–1945, a world black literature was fashioned that cemented the identity of the New Negro and an international community as his audience. Moreover, these movements laid intellectual foundations for the struggles for African independence in our time.[4] My discussion of the theme of community in modern black fiction emphasizes three novels which examine parameters for this world black community and the moral value it sustains for the ultimate freedom of the individual *and* his race. The novels, broadly representative of the three literary movements, share themes and influences: *Batouala* (1921), by René Maran; *Banjo* (1929), by Claude McKay; *Masters of the Dew* (1945), by Jacques Roumain.[5] Each of these novels questions the black man's relationship to Western Civilization, exposes the destruction of African and New World societies by imperial Europe or America, and posits some alternative whereby blacks may find themselves again in a community of free men.

One of the most controversial works of its time, *Batouala* received the Prix Goncourt in 1921. The recognition accorded Maran was mixed, yet it legitimized black literary expression on an international scale. The wide circulation of the book meant that a larger audience had access to Maran's work and that of other black writers in the future. It could also provide an arena for shared literary expression. *Batouala* initiated dialogue across cultural and linguistic lines.

The novel depicts tribal life during the colonial administration of French Equatorial Africa. Maran, a native of Martinique and reared in France, worked for the administration. He "learned the language of the country and often listened to the natives talk among themselves without their knowing. . . . He understood that the complaints of the natives weren't unfounded."[6] Maran gave voice to those complaints in his preface:

> Civilization, civilization, pride of the Europeans, and their burying ground for innocents; . . .
> You build your kingdom on corpses. Whatever you may want, whatever you may do, you act with deceit. At your sight, gushing tears and screaming pain. You are the might which exceeds right. You aren't a torch, but an inferno. Everything you touch, you consume . . . (8–9)

From 1921 until 1938, when Maran published the definitive edition of *Batouala*, and even thereafter, he incurred the wrath of many French critics and the admiration of younger African writers. The novel, itself, argues no polemic. The author comments: "It doesn't even try to explain; it states facts. It doesn't show indignation; it records" (7–8). But in its precise detail of everyday life in this African region, the novel contrasts the African world view to the European one. For the first time from a black perspective, as even Ernest Hemingway was quick to acknowledge, we "smell the smells of the village . . . eat its food . . . see the white man as the black man sees him."[7]

In the traditional society of Ubangui-Shari, Batouala, the chief, calls his villages together to celebrate the feast of Ga'nza, the ceremony of circumcision of the boys and excision of the girls. As the village prepares for the feast, Bissibi'ngui, a young warrior, tries to seduce Yassigui'ndja, Batouala's first and most prized wife. They consummate their affair publicly in the dance of love which draws the entire region into one carnal ritual. The celebration is suddenly broken by the white commandant who has forbidden the ceremony, the sudden death of Batouala's father during the uproar, and Batouala's fierce jealousy at finding himself cuckolded. Although perversions are permitted by custom in the Ga'nza celebration, Batouala is enraged by his wife's public infidelity. Enduring his grief alone, he then plots revenge against Bissibi'ngui, which results, ironically, in his own death.

"That is all there is to the story," Hemingway's review continued. "But when you have read it, you have been Batouala, and that means it is a great novel." Fortunately, there is more to this "véritable roman negre" than Batouala himself or the plot of an African love story. Although the novel is concerned with a fictional representation of tribal life and custom, it also examines what threatens to destroy that life: the younger Bissibin'gui who deposes Batouala, and the colonial whites who contribute to the breakup of traditional society. According to Batouala, African life has its own subtle value: "To live from day to day without remembering yesterday, without worrying about tomorrow, not anticipating: that is excellence, that is perfection" (17). The whites, Batouala argues, "have made the zest for living disappear in the places where they have taken up residence"

(72). The changes European colonization has made in this region are not described with the same haunting impact as in Chinua Achebe's more recent novel *Things Fall Apart*, but the threats to the stable, tradition-bound community are as severe.

Custom is the total experience of life in this community. And Batouala as chief is the guardian. "He remained faithful to the traditions which his ancestors had passed on to him, but didn't go deeply into anything outside of that. If anything were in opposition to custom, all reasoning was useless" (23). By their intrusion, colonial whites defy tradition. The Africans grumble, "we should have massacred the first one who came to our land" (70), and yearn for the times when they knew peace, not oppression: "They used to be happy in other times, before the arrival of the 'boundjous.' Working a little, and only for oneself, eating, drinking and sleeping; at long intervals some bloody ceremonies when they took out the livers of the dead in order to eat their courage and to absorb it—those were the only tasks of the blacks in other times, before the arrival of the whites" (76). Intrusion upon these rituals and beliefs signals the probable end to traditional society. Also, the violation of tradition on the part of native Africans may suggest how obsolete those values have become in the modern era. The plight of Yassigui'ndja and Bissibi'ngui indicates this second level of conflict.

Yassigui'ndja defies tradition when she is blamed for the sudden death of Batouala's father and refuses to submit to trial by ritual. According to custom, man was born to live. "If one dies it must be because someone has made a 'yorro' or uttered incantations" (98). Batouala's other wives, envious of her beauty and position, denounce Yassigui'ndja. She asks her lover Bissibi'ngui to leave the village with her. He would find work as a "tourougou," an agent of the commandant, and collect taxes from the other chiefs. Yassigui'ndja implores: "Let's leave! I don't want to take poison. I don't want to plunge my hands into boiling water. I don't want my loins to shrivel under the bite of a hot iron. I don't want my eyes to die. I don't want to die. Young, healthy, robust, I can live for many more rainy seasons" (107–8).

Just as Yassigui'ndja is implicated in the death of Batouala's father, one expects that Bissibi'ngui will be similarly implicated when Batouala dies from the wounds of a panther during a hunt—a hunt which, according to custom, is the struggle between the two men over Yassigui'ndja. The adulterous lovers must atone for their infidelity and probable murder in a ritual determined by the community to uphold its morality. Colonization, however, undercuts the process through which a divisive tribe might heal itself by offering an alternative identity for the victims. Instead of subjecting themselves to a ritual which may cause their death or vindication, Yassigui'ndja and Bissibi'ngui opt to leave the community for jobs as agents of the colonizer. Thus at the moment of Batouala's death, which is the symbolic tragedy of traditional African civilization, the lovers discover individuality, a concept alien to traditional African thought: "Alone in the world and masters of their destiny, nothing could prevent them from belonging to each other from now on" (148). As Batouala rises feebly from his deathbed in one last gesture of revenge, but falls finally to the ground "heavily, as a large tree falls," Yassigui'ndja and Bissibi'ngui have "already fled in the night" (149).

More surprising than the decline of African society or the characters' search for individuality is that these individuals will carry out the destruction of African life which colonial whites have only initiated. Outcasts such as Bissibi'ngui serve colonial interests. He resolves:

Let the hunts finish. Right after that, I shall go to Bangui to join the tourougou service, to become a militiaman as the whites say, with a rifle, cartridges, and a big knife hung on his left side by a leather belt. He wears a red tarboosh. He is paid every month. And every

Sunday . . . he goes to enjoy a little leave in the villages, where women
admire him . . .

. . . instead of paying taxes, it is we who help collect them. We do
that by ransacking both the taxable villages and those who have paid
their due. We have the rubber worked and recruit the men . . .

Such is the work of the militiaman. . . . Those little satisfactions
make the tourougou's life sweet, pleasant, easy, indeed delightful,
even more so because the commandants hardly know the language
of the country they are administering, that is to say, our country and
our language. (108)

Having access to their village's language and customs and the colonial
regime as well, Bissibi'ngui and Yassigui'ndja become masters of their
destiny, yet betray the communal values of their African home.

Maran's exposé is tempered by his non-African background and
his rather full assimilation of European culture. But working for the
colonial administration for thirteen years, he was able to observe both
traditional society and the destructive influence of the French regime.
His characterization of Batouala and the young lovers is ambivalent.
The novel exposes the abuses of colonization, but finally, not colonization itself; it appeals to the "equity and justice of the French community" to correct those abuses.[8] In the novel's intended objectivity,
conflicts are presented without neat resolution and neither character
is more heroic than the other. Nevertheless, the conflicts outlined
(traditional Africa v. modern colonial civilization, adulterous love v.
tribal custom and fidelity) had a tremendous impact on black writers everywhere, many of whom shared Maran's ambivalence for both
Africa and imperial Europe, such as Countee Cullen in his poem,
"Heritage." But there is little wonder why younger African and Afro-
American writers would rally around Maran: "He was the first black,
in France, to dare tell the truth about certain methods of colonization,

to reveal the true mentality of blacks and what they thought of European occupation."[9]

The tensions of custom, community, and international politics in the novel initiated a dialogue among black writers throughout the world. W. E. B. Du Bois, writing in the landmark Renaissance anthology, *The New Negro*, stated that: "Maran's attack on France . . . marks an era. Never before have Negroes criticized the work of the French in Africa."[10] Charles Chesnutt commented that while Maran "is not a U.S. Negro, I think his triumph is one of which all those who share the blood of his race . . . may well be proud."[11] And Léopold Senghor, one of the founding poets in the Négritude movement, wrote, "it is only with René Maran that the West Indian writers freed themselves from docile imitation of the Metropole."[12] Black writers could no longer escape conditions in Africa or the policies of Europe. Maran paved the way for writers of the diaspora to deal realistically with their past and racial heritage; he became a link "between the English and French speaking black universe between the two world wars."[13]

For the writers of the Harlem Renaissance, *Batouala* had special significance. Countee Cullen's poem, "The Dance of Love," included in his first collection, *Color* (1925), was subtitled in parenthesis, "After reading René Maran's 'Batouala.'" The poem begins:

*All night we danced upon our windy hill,*
*Your dress a cloud of tangled midnight hair,*
*And love was much too much for me to wear*
*My leaves; the killer roared above his kill,*
*But you danced on, and when some star would spill*
*Its red and white upon you whirling there,*
*I sensed a hidden beauty in the air;*
*Though you danced on, my heart and I stood still.*

Cullen draws from the ritual described by Maran in order to voice his own sensuality mingled with an American puritan ethic. Through the dance the speaker is united with his love: "We flung ourselves upon our hill and slept."[14] Cullen had a thorough knowledge of French and most likely read the novel when it first appeared. Another Renaissance francophile, Jessie Fauset, praised the novel in two book reviews which appeared in the *Crisis* in 1922. Claude McKay, who spent most of the years attributed to the Renaissance abroad, frequented Maran's salon. The exchange there may have led McKay to comment, almost prophetically, in 1932 before the appearance of *L'Etudiant Noir* that: "Negroid Africa will produce in time its own modern poets and artists peculiar to its soil."[15] Maran's importance for McKay can also be seen in *Banjo*, published in 1929. The protagonist, Ray, a Haitian, meets a Martiniquan student with aristocratic pretensions. When Ray questions him about *Batouala* the student replies that its sale was banned in his country, yet hastens to add "it was a naughty book, very strong, very strong" in order to defend the censure. This incident further educates Ray about the differences among West Indians and helps him to overcome them in his own progress toward racial awareness.

Ray's racial and cultural education is the unifying thematic element in *Banjo*. The novel, subtitled "a story without a plot," centers around the picaresque adventures of beachcombing vagabonds in Marseilles. The leader, if there is in fact *one* leader, is Lincoln Agrippa Daily, otherwise known as Banjo because of the instrument he plays. The novel outlines a man's search for a community which will unite the exotic, spontaneous impulses of life with the more distanced, sober, intellectual reflections. The two main characters, Banjo and Ray, embody these qualities respectively. Through Banjo, Ray is initiated into a community composed of the poor black rejects from Europe, Africa, and America. These are the men of the Quartier Reverve, affectionately known as the "Ditch." Through the unity established among them, a composite black hero emerges, who, like Ray, is able to define his relationship to an African cultural past and a New World future. To understand the full extent of Ray's detachment from his race, we must go to McKay's first novel, *Home to Harlem* (1928). Here we first meet Ray, a Haitian student, working his way through school as a pullman car waiter. He befriends Jake Brown, army deserter, carefree lover of many women and the good life of Harlem speakeasies. Through the friendship between them, McKay sets up a dialectic between civilization and primitivism, and the two characters, as in *Banjo*, represent these aspects respectively. Within Ray, McKay treats the problem of cultural dualism. Ray feels attracted and repelled by the spontaneity of life that Jake enjoys so naturally. Ray's education distances him from the common lot of black Americans, and his race distances him from full participation in the mainstream culture. A night of drinking on a pullman run reveals the contrast between Jake and Ray and Ray's interior distress: "Jake fell asleep as soon as his head touched the dirty pillow. Below him, Ray lay in his bunk, tormented by bugs and the snoring cooks. The low-burning gaslight flickered and flared upon the shadows. The young man lay under the untellable horror of a dead-tired man who wills to sleep and cannot" (151). The center of Ray's malaise is his inability to realize a source of kinship with blacks in America:

> Ray fixed his eyes on the offensive bug-bitten bulk of the chief. These men claimed kinship with him. They were black like him. Man and nature had put them in the same race. He ought to love them and feel them (if they felt anything). He ought to if he had a shred of social morality in him. They were all chained together and he was counted as one link. Yet he loathed every soul in that great barrack-room, except Jake. Race . . . why should he have and love a race?

Race and nations were things like skunks whose smells poisoned
the air of life. Yet civilized mankind reposed its faith and future in
their ancient, silted channels. Great races and big nations! There was
something mighty inspiriting in being the citizen of a great strong
nation ... Something the black man could never feel nor quite
understand. (154)

Exiled from his native Haiti because of American occupation, Ray
feels impotent. Part of his bitterness towards American blacks is the
extent to which he identifies them with the occupation forces. But
Ray must learn that black Americans are oppressed at home by the
same power that justifies American imperialism: "He remembered
when little Haiti was floundering uncontrolled, how proud he was
to be the son of a free nation. He used to feel condescendingly sorry
for those poor African natives; superior to ten millions of suppressed
Yankee 'coons.' Now he was just one of them and he hated them for
being one of them" (155). Through Jake, Ray expands his New World
identity.

Ray's dilemma is very close to McKay's. Although much of the
novel's exposition comes through Ray's perception—and this is also
the case in *Banjo*— he is not simply McKay's mouthpiece. Rather,
through Ray, McKay comes to understand himself and other blacks
similarly estranged: "My damned white education has robbed me of
much of the primitive vitality, the pure stamina, the simple unswag-
gering strength of the Jakes of the Negro race."[16]

Ray learns from Jake how to enjoy Harlem in its best and worst character. He must immerse himself in it, down to the bottommost rungs
in order to connect with his fullest emotions, however contradictory
they may be: "Going to Harlem ... Harlem! How terribly Ray could
hate it sometimes. Its brutality, gang rowdyism, promiscuous thick-
ness. Its hot desires. But, oh, the rich blood-red color of it! The warm

accent of its composite voice, the fruitiness of its laughter, the trailing surprises of its jazz. He had known happiness, too, in Harlem, joy that glowed gloriously upon him like the high-noon sunlight of his tropic island home" (267). Ray's ambivalence about Harlem, about being black in a color-conscious Western Civilization, helps him resolve to become a writer. By observing lives which reflect upon his own, and giving that pain a voice, perhaps Ray would realize a community to which he belonged. Unlike Jake, Ray "drank in more of life than he could distill into active animal living. Maybe that was why he felt he had to write" (265). Ray's full identity as a writer emerges in *Banjo*. Jake is replaced by Banjo, "a great vagabond of lowly life," who helps Ray articulate his identity in a new black community.

*Banjo* is not merely a continuation of bawdy Harlem set in a foreign port town. Here the vagabonds come from all parts of the world, and rather than lean on national identity (as the partying blacks in New York do), these men rely on their basic survival instincts and the brotherhood which poverty and exile bring. In the Ditch, the men survive best in groups where they might be fed by the cook on a docked ship, discover a wine keg, play music, or share living quarters. Alone, they risk barroom brawls, venereal disease, tuberculosis, murder by an angry prostitute or her pimp. Man's search for community in his most extreme need binds the characters of the Ditch. In this "international beehive," Ray finds blacks not too different from himself, from the lowest vagabond to the most assimilated Martiniquan. The national identity as a Haitian which set him apart from Harlem blacks, Jake, Zeddy, and Congo Rose, does not apply in the Ditch. And Ray discovers how all blacks are unfortunate waifs of Western Civilization, but in their abandonment and poverty there is life, color, music, language. Ray touches all of these: "In no other port had he ever seen congregated such a picturesque variety of Negroes. Negroes speaking civilized tongues, Negroes speaking all the African dialects, black Negroes, brown Negroes, yellow Negroes. It was as if every country of the world had sent representatives drifting into Marseilles. A great vagabond host of jungle-like Negroes trying to scrape a temporary existence from the macadamized surface of this great Provençal port" (68).

In the Ditch of Marseilles, "Europe's best back door," that great port along the Mediterranean where the European and African worlds meet, Ray and Banjo, "a child of the Cotton belt," join up with Senegalese Dengel, West Indian Malty Avis, Ginger, and the Arab-Oriental mulatto Latnah. Banjo's love for music and his dream of forming an orchestra (itself symbolic of a unity of disparate instruments) provides order to the chaos of bumming and some semblance of plot. The love of wine, music, food, money, and adventures bring the characters together in a common search for each of these. Just as dance and ceremony consolidated Batouala's chiefdom, barroom dancing and musical improvisation join the men and women of the Ditch: "'Beguin,' 'jelly-roll,' 'burru,' 'bombé,' no matter what the name may be, Negroes are never so beautiful as when they do that gorgeous sublimation of the primitive African sex feeling. In its thousand varied patterns, depending so much on individual rhythm, so little on formal movement, this dance is the key to the African rhythm of life . . ." (105).

Ray looks to find in his writing the same binding rhythmic force of the dance. He discovers that storytelling, in its most folkloric manner, unites the men of the Ditch as much as music and dance when they gather to trade yarns. As Ray becomes quite fully the writer/artist of this composite ethnic community, he finds his literary voice:

> . . . If I am a real story-teller, I won't worry about the complexion of those who listen and those who don't. I'll just identify myself with those who are really listening and tell my story . . . a good story,

in spite of those who tell it and those who hear it, is like good ore that you might find in any soil—Europe, Asia, Africa, America. The world wants the ore and gets it by a thousand men scrambling and fighting, digging and dying for it. The world gets its story the same way. (115)

Oral verbal communication, like music and dance, assumes a classic integrative value in this community. These cultural forms which unite the beach boys inform Ray, as well, of the false, unnecessary tension between what is civilized and what is primitive. For Ray, Banjo and the beach boys are primitive in that they follow their instinct and natural *joie de vivre*. The story within this continual celebration of life is Ray's initiation into the primitive side of himself which he has suppressed, in part, for intellectual achievement. Through Banjo, the dispossessed Africans and the West Indians, Ray learns how civilization will continually oppress and ostracize him. He saves himself by rediscovering his composite racial identity. From this confrontation, largely within himself, and his friendship with the beach boys, Ray can assert himself in the argument with the fully assimilated Martiniquan student towards the end of the novel:

You must judge civilization by its general attitude toward primitive peoples, and not by the exceptional cases. You can't get away from the Senegalese and other black Africans any more than you can from the fact that our forefathers were slaves. . . . We educated Negroes are talking a lot about a racial renaissance. And I wonder how we're going to get it. On one side we're up against the world's arrogance—a mighty cold hard white stone thing. On the other the great sweating army—our race. It's the common people, you know, who furnish the bone and sinew and salt of any race or nation. In the modern race of life we're merely beginners. If this renaissance we're talking about is going to be more than a sporadic and scabby thing, we'll have to get down to our racial roots to create it. (200)

And when the student refuses to go "back to savagery," Ray declares: "Getting down to our native roots and building up from our own people . . . is not savagery. It is culture" (200).

What Ray discovers through the vagabonds, McKay himself discovered through years of wandering. But once in Marseilles, as it had been in North Africa, "it was a relief [for him] to live in among a great gang of black and brown humanity. . . . It was good to feel the strength and distinction of a group and the assurance of belonging to it."[17] But McKay never relinquished those traits which made him unique: his essential cultural dualism, which, favorably, is a peculiarity among people of all New World societies due to the cultural syncretism between African, Indian, and European civilizations out of which the New World was born. McKay wrote: "Whatever may be the criticism implied in my writing of Western Civilization, I do not regard myself as a stranger but as a child of it. . . . I am as conscious of my new-world birthright as of my African origin, being aware of the one and its significance in my development as much as I feel the other emotionally."[18]

Through the culture of the common people Ray distills from this great variety, he learns how to survive. He takes from the Ditch what will strengthen him and his art. He leaves with Banjo at the close of the novel for parts unknown. But an important change has taken place. Ray has found himself by recognizing his birthright:

The Africans gave him a positive feeling of wholesome contact with racial roots. They made him feel that he was not merely an unfortunate accident of birth, but that he belonged to a race weighed, tested, and poised in the universal scheme. They inspired him with confidence

in them. Short of extermination by the Europeans, they were a safe
people, protected by their own indigenous culture [and] . . . defended
by the richness of their fundamental racial values. (320)

McKay has reversed our notion of the Ditch as the bottommost rung
of society by imbuing it with worthy values of community, brotherhood, and regeneration. Ray personifies a composite hero drawn
from Africa, America, and the Caribbean. We can well imagine him
as a latter-day Bissibi'ngui, who, having rebelled against the strictures
of traditional African society and experiencing the negative results of
colonization, finally rejects imperial Europe and its label of inferior-
ity. Perhaps this broad theme in *Banjo* led Du Bois to find in it an
"international philosophy of the Negro race."[19]

Continuing our thematic study of the community and its hero we
shall view Manuel Jean-Joseph, the protagonist of Jacques Roumain's
*Masters of the Dew*,[20] as an extension of Ray. The hero learns the values
of community and racial progress abroad (Roumain was educated in
Paris, Switzerland, Germany, and Spain; Manuel worked as a laborer
in Cuba) and returns home. He engages in a spectacular mission of
redemption for the individual and his community—a theme of exile
and return that nourishes both man and nation.

Complex individual fate and the problem of human redemption are central to Roumain's novel. The author argues that man
must fulfill the fate which both his religion and his community
have revealed to him in order to become a master of his land, his
people, and himself. Manuel Jean-Joseph's destiny leads him back
to his native Haiti, after fifteen years in the cane fields of Cuba, to
find a source of water to irrigate the desolate fields in his village. In
fulfilling this mission, Manuel saves his community. And in his final
martyrdom, he points the way to both an individual and collective
salvation.

Roumain reveals this theme by presenting a compact synthesis of the political and the religious life in Haiti, and embodying it in the character and spirit of Manuel. The hero emerges as a spiritual agent of social change and moral redemption. He is both man and god, sufferer and redeemer. Manuel and his community undergo a symbolic *rite de passage* from an individual to a group consciousness for liberation. Moreover, Manuel is the medium through which this liberation is achieved.

Haitian writers have often used religious iconography to express the spirit of their people. There, Christianity and traditional African religions fuse into the national religion of Voudou, which remains basically African in its language and mythology. According to ethnologist Jean Price-Mars, one of the first Haitian scholars to study indigenous culture, Voudou borrows its sacred language from Dahomey, Nigeria, and the Congo just as the Catholic religion borrows its canon from Rome.[21] Similarly, Haitian literature develops as a syncretistic neo-African literature. In the literal and figurative meaning of the work, we can identify African beliefs. The characters in Roumain's novel can be viewed in light of this symbolic frame in order to illuminate the spiritual meaning in the narrative. This method helps to identify *Masters of the Dew* as an allegory of Haitian folk religion, and as Roumain's greatest literary achievement. Manuel embodies the spirit and destiny of his people in order to reveal to them the path they must take to freedom from an otherworldly Christianity that enslaves and impoverishes them.

Turning to the novel itself, we find that Roumain's goal is not the familiar Marxist or Western dialectic common in religion and politics, but a synthesis. Although Roumain became a communist and leader of the Haitian Communist Party following the withdrawal of American occupation forces in the mid-1930s, Roumain used his first contact with Haitian peasants through the indigenist movement as a way of adapting his leftist ideology to the culture he describes. Manuel, as both man and loa, peasant and politician, becomes representative of indigenous folk tradition and political self-consciousness. The fusion of these two ideologies is necessary for collective advancement.

Misery and boredom establish the opening scene in *Masters of the Dew*. Manuel's parents have resigned themselves to a life of extreme poverty and spiritual decline. The earth has dried up, money has become scarce, and rain will not come. Their prayers to a remote Christian God are useless for Bienaimé because "so many poor creatures call continually upon the Lord that it makes a big bothersome noise. When the Lord hears it, he yells, 'What the hell's all that?' and stops up his ears. Yes, he does, leaving man to shift for himself" (23).

In the opinion of these peasants, God has not only abandoned man, but created suffering in the first place. The only hope that remains for the mother, Délira, is that Manuel will return home before she dies. Here her prayers are not to a Christian God, but to Papa Legba. She entreats: "O Master of the crossroads, open to him a road without danger" (34). About the same time the village neighbor, Clairemise, has a dream which reveals "a black man, a very old man. He was standing on the road where it crosses the path of macaw trees, and he said to me, 'Go and find Délira.' . . . Maybe it was Papa Legba" (46). Upon Roumain's suggestion of divine intervention, the manner in which African gods enter the lives of men through dreams, Manuel returns home.

He enters the village strolling "toward a mound crowned with macaw trees . . . he wanted to embrace the countryside from above, to see the plain spread out before him and glimpse, through the trees, the thatched roofs and irregular fields and gardens" (35). At once, Manuel reaches the crossroad outside his village which is guarded spiritually by Legba. Symbolically, it is only at crossroads such as this where the human and the divine axes meet that contact with the divinities takes place. It is here, perhaps, that Manuel meets Legba. Manuel notices that he has forgotten nothing of his country as familiar odors greet him. All the barriers in nature appear to open. He is one with the land.

Legba, in Haitian mythology, is "the interpreter of the gods, who translates the requests and prayers of men into their language. In Haiti he has the function of opening the barriére that separates men from the loas."[22] This description of Legba as intermediary is perhaps our most important link between the literal character of Manuel as a man, and the more symbolic representation of him as god. As the novel develops, Manuel experiences an apotheosis. He interprets the will of the gods to his fellows, opens the barrier between the two feuding families in the village, and establishes a unity among men and a corresponding unity with the gods.

Manuel teaches his first important lesson to his family. He chastises his mother, Délira, for mistreating the land:

> . . . the earth is a battle day by day without truce, to clear the land, to plant, to weed and water it until the harvest comes. Then one morning you see your ripe fields spread out before you under the dew and you say—whoever you are—'*Me—I'm master of the dew!*' and your heart fills with pride. But the earth's just like a good woman: if you mistreat her, she revolts. I see that you have cleared the hills of trees. The soil is naked, without protection. It's the roots that make friends with the soil, and hold it. It's the mango tree, the oak, the mahogany that give it rainwater when it's thirsty and shade it from the noonday heat. That's how it is . . . (45)

Man has mistreated, indeed raped nature for material benefit. Now she revolts with soil erosion and dry spells. Manuel observes, "It's not

God who betrays us. We betray the soil and receive his punishment: drought and poverty and desolation" (45).

This revelation is one step in the spiritual possession of Manuel. It also sets the stage for the redemption of all the peasants through the important discovery of water. Water, in Haitian folklore, is the home of several gods; through it man communes with them. Water is also a symbol of rebirth. Manuel clarifies this message of nature for his community. He tells them it is their duty to respond to nature's warning. They must fulfill their human destiny by becoming masters in their own right. Otherwise they will wither like the weeds and die: "You pray for rain, you pray for a harvest, you recite the prayers of the saints and the *loas*. But providence—take my word for it—is a man's determination not to accept misfortune, to overcome the earth's bad will every day, to bend the whims of the water to your needs. Then the earth will call you, 'Dear Master.' The water will call you 'Dear Master.' And there's no providence but hard work, no miracles but the fruit of your hands" (54). Thus directing his community to fulfill its responsibility as a group of workers, "masters," Manuel reaffirms his own commitment to the earth: "Growing things, my growing things! To you I say 'Honor!' You must answer, 'Respect,' so that I may enter. You're my house, you're my country. Growing things, I say, vines of my woods. I am planted in this soil, I am rooted in this earth. To all that grows, I say 'Honor.' Answer 'Respect,' so that I may enter" (55–56). finding water to irrigate the village is a matter of life or death, salvation or destruction. Manuel's mission is to lead his people not only to a spring, but to a renewed communion with the earth that will guarantee the community's survival.

On the religious level, the search for a spiritual community is also important. It is described within the actual Voudou ceremony. In the ritual of Thanksgiving for Manuel's safe arrival, the houngan becomes possessed by Legba and says, "I see that your affairs are going badly with this drought. But that will change, that will pass. . . . I, Legba, I'm master of this crossroad. I'll help my Creole children find the right road. They will leave behind this road of misery" (66). But this message only indicates the first level of struggle. More is required. Another spirit, Ogoun, the fearful loa, "god of the black-smiths and god of killers," addresses Manuel directly:

*Bolada Kimalada! O Kimalada!*
*We'll dig the canal! Ago!*
*We'll dig a canal, I say! Ago ye*
*The vein is open, the blood flows.*
*The vein is open, the blood flows! Ho!*
*Bolada Kimalada! O Kimalada!* (70)

Manuel's fate is sealed. He is the leader with a two-fold purpose. He accomplishes the first by discovering an underground source beneath a fig tree, but the second task is more costly. He must reunite his village already split by a long and violent family feud in order to get everyone's cooperation in digging the canal.

The success of Manuel's mission depends on each man doing his part. Through his love for Annaise, Manuel joins the two feuding families, but their union is a dangerous one. It costs Manuel his life at the hands of Gervilen who attacks him at night. Dying of his wounds, Manuel learns the final painful lesson needed to unify his people, to open the barriers among themselves and between them and the gods: "You've offered sacrifices to the loas. The blood of chickens and young goats you've offered to make the rain fall. That hasn't done any good—because what counts is the sacrifice of a man, the blood of a man" (158). He admonishes his mother to tell the village leader where water is, but he never tells her the name of his assassin which would only continue the feud. Death is the last barrier that

Manuel breaks open; he secures reconciliation in his secret so that "life can start all over again, so that day can break on the dew" (158). He tells his family to "sing my mourning with a song of *coumbite*," which is the system of cooperative labor that will bring prosperity to the village.

Manuel's martyr death gives the members of his community new responsibilities for maintaining unity. Délira delivers to the village leaders information on where the water is. Annaise's duty is to Manuel's child. "He loved me and I loved him," she tells Délira, "Our paths crossed." Through the unity of family and village, Manuel has secured his individual redemption and immortality. And each man's further fulfillment of his individual fate becomes the prerequisite for the redemption and liberation of the entire community. Manuel has opened the path. At the crossroad of life and death, Manuel, as loa, has achieved a unity between man and the gods. He now offers that same harmony, implicit in the continual pattern of life, death, and immortality to his countrymen. They, too, must be saved. The ending of *Masters of the Dew* is an important beginning for all New World societies.

The pattern of identity we find developing from Batouala and Bissibi'ngui, to Ray, Jake, and Banjo, and finally to Manuel, is indicative of the historical development of world African-American literature. *Batouala* did much to free francophonic African and Caribbean writers from a colonial mentality, as *Banjo* did by demanding a broader moral and cultural awareness from writers of the Harlem Renaissance. Similarly, Jacques Roumain related much of his European education and Marxist ideology to very specific problems in his native land as the artist/hero returns home.

In the character of Manuel, African man has reached a new synthesis—a spiritual harmony in the New World which is essential to sustaining the African-American way of life. He has achieved immortality through the collective advancement of his village community. He has achieved a unity with the divine forces so that the individual and the community together are redeemed.

Manuel's character, as it represents this synthesis, also represents the syncretistic nature of neo-African literature and philosophy—a fusion of African thought and New World cultural forms. For Jacques Roumain, the emphasis is on the more dominant African world view which the peasants guard in their religion and folklore where European influences tread very cautiously; or, for McKay, the lore of the low-life robust characters in Vieux Port, Marseilles.

Manuel Jean-Joseph is a new heroic figure—a revolutionary defined in a new language and symbolic structure beyond the immediate African tradition which identified Batouala or European colonization that attracted Bissibi'ngui and that rejected Ray. In the figure of Manuel, the hero has returned to the life and lore of the common people through which he saves himself and them.

The thematic development which encompasses these characters, their respective quests and initiations, leads us to an important assessment of the idea of community in world black literature. Out of the historical movements already cited, each writer has related literature as a cultural expression from incidents which have raised the level of consciousness of the victims: whether American occupation in the Caribbean, French imperialism in Africa, or the two world wars. Each event necessitated a global vision for the writers to assess change and respond to it in order for the black presence to become, in the words of Alain Locke, a "conscious contributor" to world culture. Writers of the African diaspora have defined their specific characteristics which distinguish the writer and his society. By also engaging readers most intensely on the tribal, familial, or regional plane of identity, they have touched universal concerns. And black writers continue to define particular national contributions to a world literature—be it African for Ousmane Sembene, Camara Laye, Chinua Achebe; Caribbean for René Depestre, Derek Walcott, George Lamming, Wilson Harris, Andrew Salkey; American for Ralph Ellison, James Baldwin, Ernest Gaines, Paule Marshall—through which the parameters of community, ethnicity, and morality are further enriched, and men continue to be free.

## Notes

1. Lilyan Kesteloot, *Les Ecrivains noirs de la langue française: naissance d'une littérature*, 4me ed. (1963; rpt. Bruxelles: Université Libre de Bruxelles, 1971), 35. This important study has recently been translated into English by Ellen Conroy Kennedy as *Black Writers in French: A Literary History of Négritude* (Philadelphia: Temple University Press, 1974). Quotations included in the present text are my own translations.

2. Michel Fabre, unpublished article, "*La Revue Indigène* et le Mouvement Nouveau Noir," 11. I am indebted to Professor Fabre for allowing me to read and quote from this forthcoming article. See also Naomi Garret, *The Renaissance of Haitian Poetry* (Paris: Présence Africaine, 1963), 106–117. Garret quotes at length an interview with Roumain by Antonio Vieux, "Entre Nous: Jacques Roumain," *La Revue Indigéne*, September 1927, 106, in which Roumain describes being a citizen of the world and sharing reciprocal influences in literatures of the twentieth century. He mentions "une florissante poésie nègre. Et originale," in the United States, "Counte Cullins [sic] par exemple."

3. Kesteloot, *Intellectual Origins of the African Revolution* (Washington, D.C.: Black Orpheus Press, 1972), 29.

4. Ibid. Kesteloot noted previously that the writers of the Harlem Renaissance were the first to express themes of Négritude and revolt. And more than the French authors, they were the true fathers of the black cultural renaissance in France. This point, made clear in her earlier work, *Les Ecrivains noirs*, bears upon her tracing the origins of ideas for independence: ". . . cette littérature américaine contient déjà en germes les principaux thèmes de la négritude et, à ce titre, on peut affirmer que les véritables péres de la renaissance culturelle nègre en France ne furent ni les écrivains de la tradition antillaise, ni les poètes surréalistes ou les romanciers français d'entre les deux guerres, mais les auteurs noirs des Etats-Unis: Ils marquerent si vivement nos écrivains dans la mesure où ils prétendent représenter toute une race et lancaient un cri dans lequel tons les noirs se reconnurent, le premier cri de révolte" (64).

5. Rene Maran, *Batouala*, trans. Barbara Beck and Alexandre Mboukou (1921; rpt. London: Heinemann Educational Books, 1972); Claude McKay, *Banjo* (1929; rpt. New York: Harvest Books, 1957); Jacques Roumain, *Masters of the Dew*, trans. Langston Hughes and Mercer Cook (1947; New York: Collier Books 1971). Subsequent page references refer to these editions.

6. Kesteloot, *Les Ecrivains noirs*, 84.

7. *Toronto Star Weekly*, March 25, 1922.

8. Maryse Conde, rev. of *Batouala*, *Présence Africaine* 87 (Third Quarter, 1973), 212–13.

9. Kesteloot, *Les Ecrivains noirs*, 84.

10. William E. B. Du Bois, "The Negro Mind Reaches Out," in *The New Negro*, ed. Alain Locke (1925; rpt. New York: Antheneum, 1975), 392.

11. Unpublished letter, Charles Chesnutt to Benjamin Brawley; March 22, 1922, Spingarn Collection, Howard University. Quoted in Michel Fabre, "René Maran: The New Negro and Négritude," *Phylon* 36:3 (September 1975), 341. This article details Maran's friendship with Alain Locke and other writers of the Renaissance.

12. Léopold Sédar Senghor, et al., *Les plus beaux Ecrits de l'Union Française* (Paris, 1947), 256–57.

13. Fabre, "René Maran," 340. For a further discussion of Maran's influence on younger Caribbean African and Afro-American writers see Fabre, "Autour de Maran," *Présence Africaine* 86 (Second Quarter, 1973), 165–72, and Kesteloot, *Les Ecrivains noirs*, 83–87.

14. *Color* (New York: Harper & Row, 1925), 19.

15. McKay, "A Negro Writer to His Critics," in *The Passion of Claude McKay*, ed. Wayne Cooper (New York: Schocken Books, 1973), 137. This article appeared in the *New York Herald Tribune Books*, March 6, 1932.

16. McKay, *A Long Way From Home* (1937; rpt. New York: Harvest Books, 1970), 229

17. Ibid., 277.

18. McKay, in *Passion*, ed. Cooper, 137.

19. *The Crisis*; July 1929, 234. I am indebted to Michel Fabre for allowing me to read his forthcoming article, "Aesthetics and Ideology in *Banjo*" in manuscript form, which makes use of Du Bois's and other reviewers' comments, as well as McKay's correspondence to his editor, to illuminate McKay's awareness of his audience when writing *Banjo*.

20. *Gouverneurs de la rosée* was originally published posthumously in 1945. Langston Hughes's friendship with Roumain began many years earlier when he traveled to Haiti with a letter of introduction from Walter White. See Hughes,

*I Wonder as I Wander* (1956; New York: Hill and Wang, 1964), 29–32. Hughes later translated several of Roumain's poems, and Roumain wrote the poem "Langston Hughes" around their common experiences. In addition to translating Roumain's novel with Mercer Cook as *Masters of the Dew*, Hughes translated the poetry of Nicholas Guillen and other black Hispanic poets. He became one of the most salient links between black writing in French, English, and Spanish and their mutual influences.

21. Jean Price-Mars, "Survivances africaines et dynamisme de la culture noire outre-Atlantique," *Présence Africaine* 8:10 (1956), 277.

22. Janheinz Jahn, *Muntu: The New African Culture*. trans. Marjorie Green (New York: Grove Press, 1961), 42.

# RIVERS REMEMBERING THEIR SOURCE

Comparative Studies in Black Literary History—Langston Hughes, Jacques Roumain, and Négritude

## I

*Your heart trembles in the shadows, like a face*
*reflected in troubled water.*
*The old mirage rises from the pit of the night*
*You sense the sweet sorcery of the past:*
*A river carries you far away from the banks,*
*Carries you toward the ancestral landscape.*
—JACQUES ROUMAIN, "When the Tom Tom Beats"

*It is not culture which binds the peoples of partially African origin now scattered throughout the world, but an identity of passions.*
—RALPH ELLISON, *Shadow and Act*

The single most resounding literary achievement of international scale in the twentieth century has been the development of Négritude, the celebration of a black consciousness through literature. Through Négritude, in its broadest meaning first coined by Aimé

Césaire,[1] an entire continent renamed itself, and by this act of language, whether indigenous or acquired through acculturation, generations of blacks dispersed throughout the world reclaimed a part of their identity as members of the African Diaspora. Writers from the Harlem Renaissance in the United States, the *Revue Indigéne* in Haiti, and *La Revue du Monde Noir* in Paris gave birth to literatures that, although established along lines of national language and culture, created an arena wherein blacks throughout the world could articulate their presence and condition. Each was a separate river remembering its source; each created a significant flow of theme and political passion ever circling the ancestral landscape, moving outward for independence and transformation of traditional oral forms of expression, and returning for renewal, regeneration, reunion with the past made present through language. Haitian poet Jacques Roumain has written:

> *Listen to those voices singing the sadness of love*
> *And in the mountain, hear that tom-tom*
> *    panting like the breast of a young black girl.*

Hearing the tom-tom cannot be wholly explained or dismissed as a passion. Nor would emphasis on this oral-aural contact establish for writers of African origin simply "an identity of passions" as Ralph Ellison has argued. In his effort to delineate an American literary landscape for himself and an American identity for black Americans, Ellison mistakenly separates feeling and form from their essential interaction in culture or art. He admits a shared feeling among Africans against racism and colonial oppression, but he too eagerly dismisses the question of form or culture that also might be shared among black writers who create, as Ellison does, a written literature from the continuous presence of the oral tradition.

James Baldwin, in a similar public statement in *Nobody Knows My Name*,[2] echoes Ellison's caution concerning the possibility of shared cultural forms among black writers. Baldwin, reporting on the First Congress of Negro Writers and Artists held at the Sorbonne in 1956, identifies his own ambivalence toward the cultural importance of an African presence in the world. From the assumed stance of an outsider, he discusses what might unite black writers in terms of feeling rather than form. He describes the delegates to the conference: "What they held in common was their precarious, their unutterably painful relation to the white world. What they held in common was the necessity to remake the world in their own image, to impose this image on the world, and no longer be controlled by the vision of the world, and of themselves, held by other people. And this ache united people who might otherwise have been divided as to what a man should be" (29). Baldwin may have been encouraged to take such a position by none other than the Martinican poet Aimé Césaire. When questioned at the same conference about the definition of Negro-African culture, Césaire responded, as Baldwin reports, that "no one is suggesting that there is such a thing as a pure race, or that culture is a racial product. We are not Negroes by our own desire, but, in effect, because of Europe. What unites all Negroes is the injustices they have suffered at European hands" (54).

Césaire, Baldwin, and Ellison establish a context for a public discussion of culture that is not reflected in the text of their works. On the public level all three confirm "an identity of passions," or a racial feeling, but shy away from acknowledging a racial form. More openly sensitive to the interrelation between feeling and form, between culture and "passion," and between the African and the European traditions was Richard Wright, who stated at that same conference: "I see both worlds from another, and third, point of view" (44). For Wright, that third point of view meant identifying himself as a black man of the Western world. And despite his misleading and exaggerated comment that the Negro is America's metaphor, Wright reveals the challenge that modern black writers have faced—the creation of a language that is faithful to the experience of blacks in the New World, a language that expresses the acculturation of traditional African and European forms and the dynamic transformation and reinvention of self that results. This cultural adaptation may, in fact, be the very essence of the American experience, for it permeates every multiethnic, multiracial society of the Western Hemisphere. Its people, to extend Baldwin's and Wright's metaphors, are those persons of color "who can speak of the West with real authority, whose experience, painful as it is, also proves the vitality of transgressed Western ideals." I would not go so far as to say "Western ideals"; rather, what proves vital is the ability of a dispossessed, captive people to re-create themselves out of culture contact and fusion, resilience and improvisation. These "American" persons of color, Baldwin continues, "could be considered the connecting link between Africa and the West, the most real and certainly the most shocking of all African contributions to Western cultural life. The articulation of this reality, however, was another matter. But it was clear that our relation to the mysterious continent of Africa would not be clarified until we had found some means of saying, to ourselves and to the world, more about the mysterious American continent than had ever been said before" (21).

Fulfilling this challenge to say, or to speak, requires that we use a language that expresses the American experience of blending and borrowing from the old worlds of Africa and Europe, that creates literature from the historical experience of the language and the peculiar cultural syncretism from which it was born. This mission for the black writer is expressed poetically by Césaire in his moving epic *Return to My Native Land*:

> I should discover once again the secret of great communications and of great combustions. I should say storm. I should say river. I should

say tornado. I should say leaf. I should say tree. I should be wet by all rains, made damp with all dews. I should roll like frenzied blood on the slow current of the eye of words like mad horses, clots of fresh children, curfews, vestiges of temples, precious stones far enough away to discourage miners. Whoever would not comprehend me would not comprehend the roaring of the tiger. . . . From looking at trees I have become a tree and my long tree-feet have dug in the ground long serpent holes presaging the pillage to come to high cities of bone

> *From thinking of the Congo*
> *I have become a Congo buzzing with forests and*
> *rivers where the whip cracks like a great flag*
> *the flag of the prophet*

The issue here entails a redefinition of black American civilizations, or, one might even say, neo-African civilizations, for the literature that develops in modern Africa, the Caribbean, and the United States reflects a continuing confrontation between oral traditions and literary models; we discover, according to Edward Brathwaite, a culture that is "not pure African, but an adaptation carried out mainly in terms of African tradition," and, further, "a literature of negritude, and with it, a literature of local authenticity."[3] The writer merges with the singer, the dancer, the tale-teller. And, as Wilson Harris has argued, "the community the writer shares with the primordial dancer is, as it were, the complementary halves of a broken stage."[4] The syncretistic locus for a comparative black experience emerges as the theme of the last stanza from Jacques Roumain:

> *Your soul is this image in the whispering water where*
> *your fathers bent their dark faces.*

*Its hidden movements blend you with the waves*
*And the white that made you a mulatto is this bit*
*  of foam cast up, like spit, upon the shore.*
*        ("When the Tom Tom Beats")*


## II

*I've known rivers ancient as the world*
*And older than the flow of human blood*
*in human veins.*
—LANGSTON HUGHES, "The Negro Speaks of Rivers"

Black America is a metaphor for the reinvention of the African self through a language that is the danced speech of its people. The quest for this language has both historical and textual significance. Both trends reveal how black literature, according to Wilfred Cartey's important study *Black Images*, is "an essential element in the process of self-discovery," a process through which the poet seeks to "remake the Negro image from within."[5] Cartey, echoing James Weldon Johnson's earlier plea for a racial idiom,[6] continues: "Surely the most important task engaging the black man in Africa or America has been the remaking of his own image out of his own identity. Black poetry . . . as a mode of modern poetry, has been evolving in direct relationship to the evolution of the black man himself" (183).

Historically speaking, the first decades of the twentieth century witnessed the progress of the black man into as full a participation in American and European society as the racist and neo-colonial structures would allow. At least he was no longer a slave. Capitalism, modernization, and world war brought a global consciousness to all people. Blacks in modern society, however, found the constrictions of class replaced by the confines of race. The black man, because of his race, was stereotyped as an exotic primitive. But as a result of this pervasive racial identification and the efforts of the United States government to protect the Monroe Doctrine by occupying areas in the Caribbean, blacks reversed the stigma of race and made it a banner for national identity and a racial joie de vivre. Like their cousins in North America, African and Caribbean students in Europe found their adoptive France unreceptive to their "racial" presence. And they soon discovered the roots of an African contribution to world civilization within their own ethnic identity.

The Harlem Renaissance occurred simultaneously with movements throughout the Caribbean. The occupation by American marines of several countries such as Haiti from 1915 to 1934 and Cuba in 1907 and 1917 inspired local intellectuals to explore indigenous culture, particularly folklore, as the basis of a national and racial identity in the face of an imposing foreign power that practiced racial discrimination. Haitian and Cuban populations, previously divided by an intraracial conflict between mulattos and blacks, found a common black identity to be a good defense against a foreign white authority. This shift in national consciousness meant that the Haitian identity was grounded in racial as well as national sources. In 1927, Jacques Roumain returned to Haiti from Europe, where he was educated, and joined with Normil Sylvain, Dominique Hippolyte, and Carl Brouard to establish La Revue Indigène, and from it the indigenist movement became a precursor to Négritude. Jean Price-Mars published his monumental Ainsi parla l'oncle (1928), a collection of essays in Haitian ethnology that established a critical index of Haitian folk life from which these writers could derive the form and content, the feeling and language, of a native literature. The literature used folk beliefs of voodoo for symbolism and the figurative language of Creole for black speech patterns. Roumain went on to write the first

Haitian peasant novel, *La Montagne ensorcelée* (1931), and culminated the genre with *Gouverneurs de la rosée* (1944).

Among Spanish writers in Cuba and Puerto Rico, Fernando Ortiz published *Glosario de afronegrismos* (1924), a compilation of African words in Cuban speech and words of Spanish origin with new Cuban meanings. In so doing, Ortiz called the attention of Cuban intellectuals to the rich source of black folklore in Cuba and may have countered the ideological effects of American occupation of Cuba in 1907 and 1917, the date of Ortiz's later work, *Hampa afrocubana*. By focusing on black speech patterns in Spanish, which used terms filled with African sonority, such as *cumbancha, simbombo, chevere, sandunga,* and *mondongo*, Ortiz paralleled Jean Price-Mars's pioneering study of the Creole language, where terms such as *vaudou, yamvalou, petro, ibo, loa,* and *merengue* identified dances of African origin and rhythm.[7] Ortiz's glossary paved the way for the magazine *La Revista de Avance*, the works of Puerto Rican poet Luis Pales-Matos (*Tuntun de pasa y griferia,* 1937), Ramon Guirao (*Poesia afro-cubana,* 1938), and the poetic achievements of Cuban Nicolás Guillén, whose volume *Motivios de son* in 1930 contained a glossary by Ortiz himself, which was no longer needed when his *Songoro Cosongo, poemas mulatos* was issued in 1931.

Ortiz and writers of *La Revista de Avance* ushered in a new generation of Hispanic writers who, like the Haitians of *Revue Indigène*, "demanded that poetry [indeed, all literature] bring into its cadence the rhythm of the spoken language"[8] and acknowledge its shared ancestry in African, Spanish, and French languages. Ortiz and Price-Mars may have served the same purpose as James Weldon Johnson in urging writers to abandon the imitative dialect of the popular plantation tradition and to create a racial idiom from within a more native poetic diction that allowed for the honest presentation of black character and theme. Following Johnson's lead, Langston Hughes created in his work what Jacques Roumain and Nicolás Guillén did in theirs—"a living transformation of a past into new artistic forms" (Cartey, 24). The rhythm and structure of the blues, like the danced speech of the Hispanic rumba and the Haitian Ra-Ra, became rubrics for a pregeneric New World literature. As Price-Mars has written: "music and dance are for the black man an organic necessity. Together they give an undefinable, yet essential source of strength to a nervous system burdened by the weight of very deep emotionalism. They color all the manners of the black man's life."[9]

## III

*Zumba mamá, la rumba y tambó*
*Mabimba, mabomba, bomba y bombo*

*Zumba mamá, la rumba y tambó*
*Mabimba, babomba, bomba y bombó*
—JOSÉ ZACARIAS TALLET, "La rumba"

The use of onomatopoeic words in the above refrain by José Zacarias Tallet gives an authentic structure, voice, and rhythm to a poem that describes the chase and eventual seduction—through the dance—of the woman Tomasa by José Encarnación. Here the poem transforms music by making it both a structural and a thematic element in the poem. It continues:

*Como baila la rumba la negra Tomasa,*
*como baila la rumba José Encarnación*
*Ella mueve una nalga, ella mueve la otra,*
*él se estira, se encoge, dispara la grupa,*

*el vientre dispara, se agacha, camina,*
*sobre el uno y el otro talón.*

*How she dances the rhumba, that black girl Tomasa,*
*how he dances the rhumba, José Encarnación.*
*She moves one buttock, she moves the other,*
*he stretches out, shrinks up, sticks out his rump,*
*the stomach thrusts out, he bends down, walks*
*on the one and then the other heel bone.*
*(Cartey, 80)*

Note how the text transforms the raw material of music and folklore. Unobtrusively, the very rhythm and language provide theme and form. The reader becomes engrossed in the music as Tomasa becomes, literally, seduced by Encarnación. The reader participates in the dramatic action of the poem, which illustrates an important textual element of our critical vision: The text itself remakes the image of the black man or woman in the specific context of an African-American syncretism. Through the text, then, we come to agree with Wilfred Cartey that "Although history, the political and economic sciences, ethnology and sociology, have done much . . . to begin to place the Negro before us, these disciplines do not match what literature has told us about the black man. This fact suggests that the task of making him known has required imagination in both cognition and perception" (182).

In this specifically literary realm, Edward Brathwaite has distinguished four kinds of New World literature that evoke the African presence: (1) a rhetorical literature, which uses Africa as a mask and only says the word "Africa" or invokes a dream of the Congo, Senegal, Niger, and other place names; (2) the literature of African survival, which "deals quite consciously with African survivals in Caribbean society" but does not reconnect them with the great tradition of

Africa; (3) the literature of African expression, "which has its root in the folk, and which attempts to adapt or transform folk material into literary experiment"; and (4) the literature of reconnection by writers who have lived in Africa and the New World and who "are consciously reaching out to rebridge the gap with the spiritual heartland."[10]

Most important of these developments, and the one most applicable to our study, is the "literature of African expression," for here the writer attempts to remake himself as he transforms folk material into literary experiment. Illustrating this process of self-discovery is Haitian Jacques Roumain, who took as models for his own literary expression the blues references of Langston Hughes, the sermons of James Weldon Johnson ("Nouveau Sermon nègre"), and his native Creole culture. Within this pattern of shared influence across linguistic lines one can speak of a cross-fertilization, an intertextuality among works of New World black literature. Not only was Roumain to learn from Hughes about the transformation of musical forms and folk material, but Hughes learned from Roumain, by translating his poetry, how to convey the peculiar Haitian assonance and sonority in English. In this respect, the poems "The Negro Speaks of Rivers" and "Guinea" present opportunities for interesting structural and thematic comparisons.

Both poems invest language with the power of transforming external folk material, atavistic reference, and the speaking voice itself. The speaker in Hughes's poem discovers a personal identity through his participation by means of language in an African past and a New World present. His racial knowledge is not abstract or romantic but grounded in personal and group behavior to create and re-create history. "I've known rivers," the poem begins, *because*

*I bathed in the Euphrates when dawns were young*
*I built my hut near the Congo and it lulled me to sleep*
*I looked upon the Nile and raised the pyramids above it.*

Action within the past gives the poem an authentic voice for the present and rescues the work from an inappropriately romantic perspective. Man actively participates in human history. He earns his identity through the creation of civilization. The history outside him—rivers "older than the flow of human veins"—becomes his through the poem's near incremental repetition of the phrase "my soul has grown deep like the rivers."

Roumain, in a similar lyrical language, charts a journey into the future based on what the speaker in "Guinea" has inherited from the past. The word "Guinea" resonates for a Haitian audience not only because it signifies Africa but also because it identifies the popular belief in Haitian folklore that upon death one will journey to Guinea and join the ancestors. The lyrical tone of the poem differs from the more religious language of James Weldon Johnson's "Go Down Death," or Sterling Brown's more colloquial "Sister Lou," but, nevertheless, it initiates Roumain's search for a figurative language to express the form and feeling of his people. The poem is descriptive of one speaker's journey and prescriptive and instructive in the imperative mood for his audience:

*C'est le lent chemin de Guinée*
*La mort t'y conduira*
*Voici les branchages, les arbres, la forêt*
*Écoute le bruit du vent dans ses longs cheveux*
*   d'eternelle nuit.*

*C'est le lent chemin de Guinée*
*Tes pères t'attendent sans impatience*
*Sur la route, ils palabrent*
*Ils attendent*
*Voici l'heure où les ruisseaux grelottent comme*
*   des chapelets d'os*

*C'est le lent chemin de Guinée*
*Il ne te sera pas fait de lumineux accueil*
*Au noir pays des hommes noirs:*
*Sous un ciel fumeux percé de cris d'oiseaux*
*Autour de l'oeil du marigot*
   *les cils des arbres s'écartent sur la clarté pourrissante.*
*Là, t'attend au bord de l'eau un paisible village,*
*Et la case de tes pères, et la dure pierre familiale*
   *où reposer enfin ton front.*

*It's the long road to Guinea*
*Death takes you down*
*Here are the boughs, the trees, the forest*
*Listen to the sound of the wind in its long hair*
   *of eternal night*

*It's the long road to Guinea*
*Where your fathers await you without impatience*
*Along the way, they talk*
*They wait*
*This is the hour when the streams rattle*
   *like beads of bone*

*It's the long road to Guinea*
*No bright welcome will be made for you*
*In the dark land of dark men:*
*Under a smoky sky pierced by the cry of birds*
*Around the eye of the river*
   *the eyelashes of the trees open on decaying light*
*There, there awaits you beside the water a quiet village,*
*And the hut of your fathers, and the hard ancestral stone*
   *where your head will rest at last.*

In the repetition of the droning phrase "C'est le lent chemin de Guinée," Roumain establishes a link to Haitian folk culture. And in his use of the "o" sound for near rhyme and rhythm, he approximates the open vowel sounds of the Creole language, as in "La mort t'y conduira."

When Langston Hughes translated the poem, he was particularly sensitive to this use of language and approximated the texture of the open, sonorous speech. Instead of the literal translation of the line to read "death will lead you there," he chose the sonorous, alliterative line "death takes you down" to maintain thematic clarity and to preserve the tonal quality of the language. The speaker in Roumain's original text, as in the translation, discovers a language through which he can experience death on the literal level and passage from the New World to Africa on the symbolic level. His experience is visual and aural: "Here are the boughs, the trees, the forest / Listen to the sound of the wind in its long hair / of eternal night." The speaker comes to know how the wind is animated, personified. And having established a primary contact with nature, he then discerns the voices of his fathers that accompany his passage through a decaying light that signifies no bright welcome. But rather than feeling an existential gloom, the speaker discovers "a quiet village" beside the water and the ancestral stone upon which he will rest. The repeated "long road to Guinea" suggests a passage that will test the speaker and, as in Hughes's "The Negro Speaks of Rivers," make his presence one of active and earned behavior until he endures the darkness of his own fears and earns the rewarding, soft darkness of eternal rest.

Roumain's voice in the poem is that of a learned observer, instructing the uninitiated, who may still need to find—in the folk belief of spiritual and cultural redemption—comfort from the psychic dislocation and abandonment of his past in the New World. By its reference to Africa, Hughes's subjective voice affirms, indirectly, the historical, the folkloric, and, directly, the spiritual journey. Roumain is still groping for language that connects more fully to this rite of passage.

Roumain and Hughes were familiar with each other's work, but when Roumain began to write he composed melancholic, meditative verse that described his feelings of alienation upon his return to Haiti from his education abroad. Roumain's early poetry shows his search for a language to illuminate Haitian reality as the poet's own national identity. Other writers of the *Revue Indigène* were helpful to him, but so were writers of the Harlem Renaissance like Hughes and Countee Cullen. When interviewed by the review, Roumain suggested that Haitian writers become more aware of the flourishing North American black poetry. Years later, Roumain described indirectly how he learned from Hughes to depict the black figurative language of the blues. Note Roumain's direct borrowing of black American speech patterns in his tribute to Hughes:

*At Lagos you knew sad faced girls*
*Silver circled their ankles.*
*They offered themselves to you naked as the night*
*Gold-circled by the moon.*

*You saw France without uttering a worn, shop-made phrase;*
      Here we are, Lafayette!
*The Seine seemed less lovely than the Congo.*

*Venice. You sought the shade of Desdemona.*
*Her name was Paola.*
*You said:* Sweet, sweet Love!

*And sometimes*
Babe! Baby!
*Then she wept and asked for twenty lire.*

*Like a Baedeker your nomad heart wandered*
*From Harlem to Dakar.*
*The Sea sounded on in your songs—sweet, rhythmic,*
    *wild . . .*
*And its bitter tears*
*Of white foam blossom-born.*

*Now here in this cabaret as the dawn draws near you*
    *murmur . . .*
Play the blues again for me!
O! for me again play the blues!

*Are you dreaming tonight, perhaps, of the palm trees, of*
    *Black Men there who paddled you down the dusks?*
            *("Langston Hughes")*

Roumain's sensitivity to colloquial speech, music, and folklore as a basis for indigenous figurative language is evident in his long, major poem, *Bois d'ébène* and surfaces again as a rhythmic device in his more political piece, "Sales Nègres" ("Dirty Negroes"):

*Well then*
*here we are*
*we negroes*
*we niggers*
*we dirty niggers*
*we won't accept it any more*
. . . . .
*that surprises you*
*after our: yes, sir*
*polishing your shoes*
*yes, father*

*to the missionary whites*
*yes, master*
*harvesting for you*
*the coffee*
*cotton*
*peanuts*
*in Africa*
*America*
*like the good negroes*
*poor negroes*
*dirty negroes*
*that we were*
*that we won't be any longer*

But the creation of the peasant novel was Roumain's greatest achievement in Haitian letters. *Gouverneurs de la rosée* (1944), translated by Langston Hughes and Mercer Cook as *Masters of the Dew* (1947),[11] shows Roumain's masterful transformation of Creole language, music, and folklore into literary experiment.

In *Masters of the Dew* we encounter the peasant greeting of "Honor," which is answered by "Respect" when one peasant visits another. Roumain transforms that dialogue in the text to indicate an exchange of greeting between Manuel, the protagonist, and his homeland of Fonds Rouge. The hero, after fifteen years of working in the cane fields of Cuba, returns to his drought-stricken village and finds water to irrigate the land. The community, however, is divided by a family feud that prevents the peasants from working cooperatively to build an aqueduct now that water is found. Roumain's use of the oral exchange "Honor-Respect" establishes an internal dialogue between Manuel and himself, and an external one with Nature, with whose life forces he renews his primal covenant and from whom he eventually gains redemption in his martyrdom and sustenance for his community:

> [Manuel] was dull of happiness despite the stubborn thoughts that haunted him. He wanted to sing a greeting to the trees: "Growing things, my growing things! To you I say 'Honor!' You must answer 'Respect,' so that I may enter. You're my house, you're my country. Growing things, I say, vines of my woods, I am planted in this soil. I am rooted in this earth. To all that grows, I say, 'Honor.' Answer, 'Respect,' so that I may enter."
> He proceeded at that long, almost nonchalant but graceful gait of a Negro of the plain, sometimes cutting a path with a swift stroke of his machete. He was still humming when he reached a clearing. (35)

Note furthermore how Manuel's exchange with nature necessitates dialogue with his fellow villagers: "Manuel began to talk to the peasants, one after the other. For years hate had become with them a habit. It had given an object and a target to their impotent anger against the elements. But Manuel had translated into good Creole the exacting language of the thirsty plain, the plaint of growing things, the promises and all the mirages of the water" (115).

By thus focusing on Roumain, we can see how the black writer re-creates language from within the specific boundaries of his native culture and speech. Moreover, Roumain's achievement—transforming specific oral, musical, and folk forms into literature—links him to Hughes in the United States, Guillén in Cuba, and Léopold Sédar-Senghor in Senegal. Oral traditions, transformed, are the cultural elements shared by these black writers. They accomplish the very dictum articulated earlier by Jean Price-Mars that "nothing will be able to prevent tales, legends, songs come from afar or created, transformed by us, from being a part of us, revealed to us as an exteriorization of our collective self."[12] And these writers of New World literature have responded in their way to Derek Walcott's contemporary caution:

> *How choose*
> *Between this Africa and the English tongue I love?*
> *Betray them both, or give back what they give?*
> *How can I face such slaughter and be cool?*
> *How can I turn from Africa and live?*
>     ("A Far Cry from Africa," In a Green Night)


## IV

Black writers of the Caribbean, North America, and Africa confront European civilization on the cultural level, not merely on the level of feeling or passion. The form of their response to acculturation has been to combine the best of traditional African oral heritage with the most useful European vocabulary. African languages in motion and in contact with Spanish, French, and English have created something different, something new—not a pidgin or dialect version, but a language that seeks within its national oral foundation a synthesis based on racial characteristics and allegiance. We must argue against Ralph Ellison's assertion that "since most of the so-called 'Negro cultures' outside Africa are necessarily amalgams, it would seem more profitable to stress the term 'culture' and leave the term 'Negro' out of the discussion." In the same spirit Ellison continues to disregard culture as an aspect of race and to mislead his readers:

> It is not culture which binds the peoples who are of partially African origin now scattered throughout the world, but an identity of

passions. We share a hatred for the alienation forced upon us by Europeans during the process of colonization and empire and we are bound
by our common suffering more than by our pigmentation. But even
this identification is shared by most non-white peoples, and while it
has political value of great potency, its cultural value is almost nil.[13]

Fortunately, the literature of the African Diaspora, whether on
the continent itself or in the West Indies, tells a different story. We
find that through the shared history of oppression racial identity and
folk life have created the means by which men acquired language: a
national language built upon the resonance of folk forms and rhythmic syntax of speech that approximated the African gift of music and
appropriated a vocabulary of convenience from Europe.

By acquiring language and imbuing it with terms directly related
to New World experience through music and folklore (indigenous
creations), black writers created a bond among themselves through
literature. Ellison and Baldwin fail, at least publicly, to make this
re-creation and reconnection vital to their work. They fail to learn
from the literary experimentation of writers like Hughes, who was
the most important cultural ambassador throughout the Diaspora
during and after the Renaissance years.

As critics, writers, and teachers of Afro-American literature we
need to return to what Hughes discovered through his translations,
personal travels, associations, and creative work, so that we too might
identify the shared cultural forms used by black writers to reconnect
to a common, ancestral resonance. This kind of cross-cultural comparative criticism can illuminate the dimensions of a black sensibility
in literature and effectively shape our understanding of literary history. Furthermore, our willingness to approach black writing by going
beyond specific geographic or historical boundaries can add to the
different ways in which survey courses are organized. By identifying

| Date | Negrissimo (Cuba, Puerto Rico) | Harlem Renaissance (U.S.A) (Harlem, Washington D.C., etc.) | Négritude (Paris, Haiti, Martinque, Senegal) |
|---|---|---|---|
| 1903 | | *Souls of Black Folk*, Du Bois | |
| 1907 | American Occupation of Havana | | |
| 1910 | | *Crisis* Magazine | |
| 1915 | | | American Occupation of Haiti (1915–34) |
| 1917 | *Hampa afrocubana*, Ortiz Second American Occupation of Cuba | | |
| 1921 | | | *Batouala*, René Maran; Prix Concourt |
| 1922 | | *American Negro Poetry*, ed. J. W. Johnson *Batouala* reviewed in *Crisis* Cullen writes "Dance of Love" | |
| 1923 | | *Cane*, J. Toomer *Opportunity Magazine* est. | |
| 1924 | *Glossary of Afro-Cubanisms*, Ortiz | | |
| 1925 | | *Color*, Countee Cullen *The New Negro*, ed. Locke | |
| 1926 | | *The Weary Blues*, Hughes | |
| 1927 | | | *La Revue Indigène*, Roumain et al. (Haiti) |
| 1928 | *La Revista de Avance* (Cuba) *La Revista de la Antilles* (Puerto Rico) | | *Ainsi parla l'oncle*, Price-Mars (Haiti) |
| 1929 | | *Banjo*, Claude McCay | |
| 1930 | *Motivios de son*, Guillen (w/ glossary by Ortiz) | | *La Revue du Monde Noir*, Nardal/Sarjous (Paris) (1930–34) |
| 1931 | *Songoro Consongo, poemas mulatos*, Guillen | | *Légitime défense*, Radical students (Paris) (1931–32?) |
| 1932 | | *Southern Road*, S. Brown | |
| 1934 | | | *L'Étudiant noir*, Damas, Césaire, Senghor (Paris) |
| 1935 | | *Mules and Men*, Z. N. Hurston | |
| 1937 | *Tuntun de pasa y griferia*, Luis Pales Matos (Puerto Rico) | | *Pigments*, L. Damas |
| 1938 | *Poesia afro-cubana*, Ramon Guirao | | |
| 1939 | | | *Cahier d'un retour au pays natal*, Césaire |
| 1940 | | *Native Son*, R. Wright | |
| 1941 | | | *Tropiques*, Césaire (Martinique) |
| 1944 | | | *Gouverneurs de la rosée*, J. Roumain (Haiti) |
| 1947 | | *Masters of the Dew*, trans. Hughes and Cook | *Chants d'ombre*, Senghor *Présence Africaine* founded |
| 1948 | | | *Anthologie de . . . poésie nègre*, ed. Senghor (Paris) |
| 1952 | | *Invisible Man*, Ellison | *Peau noire, masques blancs*, Fanon (Paris) |
| 1956 | | | First Congress of Negro Artists and Writers (Paris) |

uses of language in terms of shared cultural forms among black writers in French, English, and Spanish, we free Afro-American literature from the confines of the North American cultural prison that automatically relegates it to minority, secondary, and thus inferior status. We also discover modes of universality within the individual text and a resonant intertextuality with literatures that share a common historical background and linguistic synthesis. In response, then, to Walcott's searing probe, "how can I turn from Africa and live?," we must answer that each New World literature is a river that remembers its source while continuing its individual direction, shape, and depth where language swims and *all* our nets pull.

## Notes

1. *Return to My Native Land*, trans. Emile Snyder (Paris: Présence Africaine, 1971). Critics have taken from Césaire a broader definition which includes "the awareness of being black, the simple acknowledgment of a fact that implies the acceptance of it, a taking charge of one's destiny as a black man, of one's history and culture." See the translator's introd. to Lilyan Kesteloot's *Black Writers in French: A Literary History of Négritude* (Philadelphia: Temple Univ. Press, 1974), xviii.

2. *Nobody Knows My Name* (New York: Dial, 1961). All further references to this work appear in the text.

3. "The African Presence in Caribbean literature," *Daedalus* 103 (1974), 78.

4. *Tradition, the Writer and Society* (London: New Beacon, 1973), 52.

5. *Black Images* (New York: Teachers Coll. Press, 1970), 24–25.

6. See Johnson, pref., *American Negro Poetry*, rev. ed. (New York: Harcourt, 1931).

7. G. R. Coulthard, quoted in Cartey, 25.

8. Cartey, 28.

9. Jean Price-Mars, quoted in Cartey, 78.

10. Brathwaite, 80–81.

11. *Masters of the Dew*, (New York: Reynal, 1947). All further references to this work appear in the text.

12. Jean Price-Mars, quoted in Cartey, 24.

13. *Shadow and Act* (New York: Signet, 1964), 255.

Part II

# WRITING
## AFRICAN AMERICAN
## CULTURAL THEORY

# THE BLACK WRITER'S
# USE OF MEMORY

This essay centers on my interest in the way geographic locations such as the American South and Africa have become important sites of memory in the construction of a viable African-American culture. In this connection, it is very significant that Pierre Nora's conception of memory-generating experiences rests on his assessment of major differences, if not stark ruptures, between history and memory.[1]

Nora sees history as static and memory as dynamic. He defines history loosely as "how our hopelessly forgetful modern societies, propelled by change, organize the past." He defines memory as an actual phenomenon, "open to the dialectic of remembering and forgetting" (8). Where history, for Nora, is the reconstruction of what no longer exists, memory is life itself, vulnerable to the vicissitudes of our time, nourishing recollection, yet responsive to trends, including censorship. Whereas history calls for analysis and criticism, memory is almost sacred, absolute, concretely rooted in "spaces, gestures, images, objects" (9). Here Nora appears to echo Joseph Campbell on the power of myth and Carl Jung on the prevalence of dream symbols and the power of the collective unconscious.

Although Nora emphasizes the analytic characteristic of history and the psychological aspects of memory, which interests those of us who, as writers, become critics of culture, he betrays something of a Eurocentric bias in favor of recorded historical analysis when he considers non-Europeans. He argues (much too disparagingly, for my taste) that "among the new nations, independence has swept into history societies newly awakened from their ethnological slumbers by colonial violation. Similarly, a process of interior decolonization has affected ethnic minorities, families and groups that until now have possessed reserves of memory but little or no historical capital" (7).

Using Nora's own criteria for the recovery of the past, I intend to show that the presence in our culture of significant *lieux de mémoire* establishes the value of cultural memory and the very kind of history or historiography that is not dependent on written analysis or criticism but rather achieves an alternative record of critical discussion through the exercise of memory. Memory becomes a tool to regain and reconstruct not just the past but history itself. What is useful in Nora's argument is his broad recognition of how *lieux de mémoire* may contribute to the process of cultural recovery.

When particular places, gestures, images, or objects deliberately call us to remember, when they project a definite will to remember— such as firework displays on the Fourth of July, the Vietnam Veterans Memorial in Washington, D.C., the AIDS quilt pieced together from individual lost lives and displayed collectively in traveling exhibits nationwide, or the Macy's Thanksgiving Day Parade featuring cartoon characters as inflated giants of our childhood fantasies—when these events call us to remember, they become *lieux de mémoire*, sites of memory. In essence, Nora argues that "the quest for memory is the search for history."

## "ONE DISREMEMBERED TIME"

When I consider the abject exclusion of African Americans from the discourse of mainstream American history, culture, or society, and when I ponder the distinct rupture in black family genealogy,

THE BLACK WRITER'S USE OF MEMORY 57

I look for what strategies of recollection have been used to transmit an Afrocentric wholeness in our heritage. I am reminded of one of my favorite poems by Robert Hayden, a major poet who died in 1981. Hayden's work includes classic historical meditations (such as his sonnet "Frederick Douglass" and his poem on the slave trade called "Middle Passage"). He also recounts in intimate, personal terms the psychological consequences of the loss of family and, by turns, memory and a name. His poem "Mystery Boy Looks for Kin in Nashville" goes like this:

Puzzle faces in the dying elms
promise him treats if he will stay.
Sometimes they hiss and spit at him
like varmits caught
in a thicket of butterflies.

A black doll,
one disremembered time,
came floating down to him
through mimosa's fancywork leaves and blooms
to be his hidden bride.

From the road beyond the creepered walls
they call to him now and then,
and he'll take off in spite of the angry trees,
hearing like the loudening of his heart
the name he never can he never can repeat.

And when he gets to where the voices were—
Don't cry, his dollbaby wife implores;
I know where they are, don't cry.
We'll go and find them, we'll go
and ask them for your name again.[2]

What is true for the psychological dislocation and disremembering in this poem becomes emblematic for the urgency of our recovery of cultural memory. And this reach exceeds the boundaries of national identity, those "creepered walls" and the cruel, taunting voices of mistaken heritage. In my reading of African-American literature I sense a movement of cumulative racial significance, from the particular to the global, from, say, Harlem, an urban district, to the South, a region of several states, and to Africa, a continent. These sites have been used by many African-American writers not only to evoke a sense of place but, more importantly, to enlarge the frame of cultural reference for the depiction of black experiences by anchoring that experience in memory—a memory that ultimately rewrites history.

Let me take you, for a moment, to the neighborhood where I now live, Harlem, in New York City. Entering my part of Manhattan from the Major Degan Thruway at the intersection of Lenox Avenue and 145th Street there are two nightclubs, one called the Zanzi-bar, the other called the Lagos Bar. Farther south Lenox Avenue becomes Malcolm X Boulevard. At the intersection of 125th Street and Malcolm X Boulevard street vendors have for many years kept an open-air market for fruits, vegetables, North Carolina pecans, cassette tapes, and dungarees. The street sign above this corner says AFRICAN MARKET SQUARE. A short walk in the vicinity brings you in contact with black people of every shade and texture, living on numbered streets and on streets that have changed their names to Frederick Douglass Boulevard, Johnny Hartman Plaza, Marcus Garvey Park, and Adam Clayton Powell Boulevard.

What you may gather from these names and places is a sense of changes within history, for these people were important in Harlem's past. But most important—especially to me, a relative newcomer to the area—is the fact that the people have taken charge of their lives and their identity as African Americans. Not only do these names

celebrate and commemorate great figures in black culture, they provoke our active participation in that history. What was important
yesterday becomes a landmark today. Invoking memory of that time
or that person is the only way to orient oneself today. If you are lost
in upper Manhattan, you must remember the people who lived there
and those who continue to live there or you will never find your direction. This is the way some people have defined their community and
themselves. This exercise and reification of cultural memory recon-
structs a history of that region that never included blacks until 1915.
Harlem, you recall, was not settled originally by blacks, nor was the
great, spacious design of urban boulevards and vintage architecture
designed for blacks, but for a wealthy white Euro-American population. Furthermore, the predominant presence of blacks in Harlem
from 1915 onward simply represented a demographic shift in the
population. Only later and through an affirmation of the lived experience of the people did changes in street names and urban character
signal the revitalization of a community into an expression of cultural
memory.

By calling themselves to remember Africa and/or the racial past,
black Americans are actually re-membering, as in repopulating
broad continuities within the African diaspora. This movement is
nonlinear, and it disrupts our notions of chronology. If history were
mere chronology, some might see Africa as the beginning of race
consciousness—and racial origin—rather than the culmination or
fulfillment of ancestry. Enslaved Africans were brought to the New
World, mainly to the American South (only later did they migrate in
great numbers to the North). But in much of the material centered in
a construction of racial culture and identity, an ahistorical, cyclical,
figurative movement emerges as the reverse. An investigation of Harlem as a northern urban community reveals direct ties—deliberate,
crafted ties—to the American South and then to Africa. And these are

not places but stages or sites on which the drama of self-acquisition is played. Take, for example, the scene in Ellison's *Invisible Man* when the nameless protagonist eats a yam purchased from a Harlem street vendor. He, of course, asserts his birthright in the delirium of his joy when he exclaims, "I yam what I am."[3] Most critics have reflected upon the affirmation of identity and cultural punning that occurs here. But further investigation reveals that with one delicious bite the protagonist is projected back to the South of his cultural conditioning and source of his present rebellion, and forward to a reassessment of racial "sites," events, or *lieux de mémoire*.

"Then you must be from South Car'lina," the vendor says with a grin. And the protagonist responds, "South Carolina nothing, where I come from we really go for yams." The protagonist exchanges place specificity for a broader reference—gustatory, culinary, and otherwise. Yet just as soon as he delights in another discovery when he reflects: "Yet the freedom to eat yams on the street was far less than I had expected upon coming to the city" (261), he ingests a bit of yam spoiled by frost. This moment of memory and revelation—almost akin to Proust's reverie with the tasty madeleine—is laden with Ellison's persistent irony in the novel, forcing the protagonist and the reader to rethink at every turn the most manifest expressions of a recaptured, remembered past. This scene of bittersweet birthright comes just before the invisible man happens upon the eviction of an elderly couple whose belongings include Free Papers and in whose defense the protagonist acts in such a way as to earn him a position with the Brotherhood. Ellison's boomeranging of expectations, a spiral of history and memory, fuels the novel. But Ellison's argument about ancestry and the validity of purely racial sources extends far back to the beginnings of African-American cultural expression.

A look at the names of black fraternal organizations, schools, and newspapers during the nineteenth century reveals a preponderance of references to Africa: The African Association for Mutual Relief (1827), the African Free School (1828) and, of course, the African Methodist Episcopal Church. These names serve two functions: (1) to acknowledge the fact of historical origin and (2) to remind members past and present of that historical origin. If family disruption and loss of precise genealogy distance black Americans from more solid, or literal, connections to an African identity, they nonetheless increase our predilection for the way figurative connections become charged with increasing symbolic importance. And here again memory rather than history becomes a fruitful strategy for the recovery of the past.

## MEMORY AS METAPHOR: "I'M STILL IN LUZANA?"

The prose tradition in African-American literature, as seen in Ellison's *Invisible Man*, contributes to Nora's argument differentiating history and memory. The conflict for black writers is crucial, for it addresses the simple issue of control of the past as well as proper transmission of the past. The presence in our literature of such distinctive genres as the slave narrative, the autobiographical novel, and the poetics of blues music suggests the subversive lengths artists have gone to preserve the personal past and project distinctive voices into the whirlwind. Ernest Gaines's novel *The Autobiography of Miss Jane Pittman* instructs us about the gains that accrue from memory's revision of history. The protagonist, Miss Jane, is important. She is a *lieux de mémoire* ripe for the promulgation of cultural memory and African ancestry, as represented by her skill at oral rather than written transmission or analysis of her story, her history. The tension between conventional history—and even the recently valued technique of oral history—and memory here suggests that Miss Jane's exercise of memory makes her into a metaphor.

When the historian arrives to hear Miss Jane's story, his efforts are thwarted by Mary, Miss Jane's neighbor. The exchange between them is telling:

> "What you want to know about Miss Jane for?" Mary said.
> "I teach history," I said. "I'm sure her life's story can help me explain things to my students."
> "What's wrong with them books you already got?" Mary said.
> "Miss Jane's not in them," I said.[4]

The record of history contained in books contrasts sharply with Miss Jane's as yet unrecorded memory. As he listens and records her story, the historian learns that without ever leaving Luzana (itself a metaphorical rendering of what Louisiana really is in folk speech, and hence a place different from the state's geographical name), Miss Jane experiences all of history (slavery, emancipation, Reconstruction, Jim Crow segregation, and the civil rights movement, and a nascent period of black power). She contains that history, carries it in her memory. Her larger historical participation makes her a metaphor of the witness of the past. Secondly, the historian learns that orality and memory transmitted orally require communal expression. When Miss Jane would fall silent, "someone else would always pick up the narration." When the historian concludes his introductory remarks he affirms, "Miss Jane's story is all of their stories, and their stories are Miss Jane's." By remaining within Luzana and remaining faithful to her individual and collective memory, Miss Jane records a new history.

If history as story promotes narrative, then memory, which is often expressed episodically and through visceral imagery independent of chronology, very much like a dream, reveals itself often as meta-phor. The tension between history and memory then can also be expressed as a tension between narrative and metaphor. If I can extend this argument into a consideration of race and gender, I want to note that the tension between the telling and receiving of Miss Jane's story owes something to the dynamic of the male historian confronting the black female memory, subject to the demands and release of a suppressed authority as a woman. I mention this aspect of the framework largely to call our attention to Gaines's fiction and to the persistent manner in which major novels by contemporary black woman writers have used similar strategies of reappropriation of the past. In Sherley Anne Williams's novel *Dessa Rose*, the memory of the slave woman must elude capture in the "history" of rebellion about to be written by Adam Nehemiah. When Dessa is able to pre-serve her name and her memory from further violation in history, she becomes a metaphor for the way a black woman's story remains her own.

More recently, Toni Morrison's novel *Beloved* argues for this same complexity when Sethe's narrative of infanticide is disrupted by the actual presence of memory in the form of her dead daughter's ghost. Morrison, like Ellison, enjoys the irony of memory associa-tions and continuous haunting. When Morrison tells readers at the novel's close "It was not a story to pass on,"[5] we are reminded of the three-hundred-odd pages of the telling, the passing on. This is the novelist's effort to heal the psychological disruption of identity Robert Hayden spoke about. With Baldwinesque urgency, Morri-son, speaking of Beloved, intones: "Everybody knew what she was called, but nobody anywhere knew her name. Disremembered and unaccounted for, she cannot be lost because no one is looking for her, and even if they were, how can they call her if they don't know her name?" (274).

## "WHAT IS AFRICA TO ME"

Tradition in black poetry, like its cousin in prose, observes the presence of racial ancestry and memory with considerable irony and surprise. If we overlook the most glaring clichés of the "African warrior o my beautiful black woman" poetry of the sixties, we learn that racial memory provoked poets as distant in time and sensibility as Phillis Wheatley, Countee Cullen, and Langston Hughes, and distantly beyond our shores to the *négritude* poetry of Aimé Césaire, Jacques Roumain, and Léopold Sédar Senghor. Here metaphor and remembrance occupy the charged terrain of cultural authority.

If Phillis Wheatley claims the moral authority that derives from African ancestry when she admonishes her Puritan audience that "Negroes black as Cain / may be refined and join th'angelic train,"[6] why has there been such a reluctance among modern black poets to use cultural memory for reclamation rather than renunciation?

Poetic practice throughout tradition has charged the word *Africa* with meaning but not memory. And mere utterance of the word cannot endow us with the living phenomenon a *lieux de mémoire* requires. Perhaps we would do better if we examined the conflicting elements of race that appeared during the years of the Harlem Renaissance when such poets as Countee Cullen and Langston Hughes were battling over the poetic prizes of cultural memory. Cullen embraced book learning, Hughes experience. Cullen treasured the written text of history, Hughes the memory of active living. Compare, for example, Cullen's lines "Africa? A book one thumbs / Listlessly, till slumber comes"[7] with the compelling *lieux de mémoire* within an unnamed Africa in Hughes's active musings in "The Negro Speaks of Rivers," written before Hughes ever traveled to the continent: "I bathed in the Euphrates when dawns were young / I built my hut near the Congo and it lulled me to sleep."[8]

Cullen's poem "Heritage" remains an enigma of cultural memory without the masterful jousting and dueling between narrative and metaphor we find in selected prose. Although Cullen's poem vacillates between acceptance and rejection of ancestry, the speaker's ambivalence fails to affirm—even ironically—the complexity of a self discovered through the art of memory. Against the speaker's repeated claims of forgetfulness toward a "heathen" Africa, an imperative of ancestry emerges in the inescapable discovery of his racial nature, "one three centuries removed." He begins:

> *What is Africa to me:*
> *Copper sun or scarlet sea,*
> *Jungle star or jungle track,*
> *Strong bronzed men, or regal black*
> *Women from whose loins I sprang*
> *When the birds of Eden sang? (36)*

Cullen attempts to counter these stereotypical and received images with the overwhelming urge to amnesia brought on by conversion to Christianity. "Unremembered are her bats / Circling through the night, her cats." Then nature intervenes to question the extent of the speaker's forgetting: "In an old remembered way / Rain works on me night and day" (36). This brings the speaker face to face with the racial and religious conflicts behind his dilemma. Memory, even in its absence, is the poet's chief means of confronting a troublesome past and an uncertain present.

How the Senegalese poet Léopold Sédar Senghor recognized Cullen's poetics of racial amnesia only to subvert them reveals the distinctive strategies this African poet used to project metaphors of remembering. Senghor's recurring master trope is "the Kingdom of Childhood," that realm of personal past he reclaims from the prejudices of Europe and baptizes as *négritude*, which he defines as the sum total of cultural values in the black world. Memory, for Senghor, is a celebration of the self. And although he acknowledges a debt to Cullen, Senghor shouts his repeated "I remember" as a proclamation and embrace of ancestral joy rather than the "unremembering" in Cullen or the "disremembering" in Hayden. These points became clear to me as I began to translate Senghor's poetry. In his poem "Joal" Senghor celebrates his birth place and, in so doing, celebrates himself:

*Joal!*
*I remember.*

*I remember the regal* signare *women under the green shade of verandas,*
*Those mulatto women with eyes as surreal as moonlight on the shore.*

*I remember the red glory of Sunset*
*Koumba N'Dofene would weave into his royal cloak.*

*I remember the funeral feasts fuming with the blood*
*Of slaughtered cattle,*
*The noise of quarrels, the rhapsodies of the griots.*

*I remember the pagan voices singing the* Tantum Ergo,
*The processions and the palm leaves and the triumphal arches.*
*I remember the dance of nubile girls,*
*The wrestling songs—Oh! the final dance of stout young men*
*Poised so slender and tall*
*And the women's pure shout of love—Kor Siga!*

*I remember, I remember . . .*
*My head swirling.*
*What a weary walk through the long days of Europe*
*Where sometimes an orphan jazz comes sobbing, sobbing, sobbing.*[9]

Senghor's choice of "Je me rappelle" in the original French for "I remember" suggests an important act of self-creation in the exercise of memory. The reflexive verb can mean literally "I myself recall" or "I recall myself," thus bringing the self into being. Senghor also ponders the redemptive power of blackness when he observes Africanness in New York City in all its racial and spiritual dimensions:

> *New York! I say New York, let black blood flow into your blood.*
> *Let it wash the rust from your steel joints, like an oil of life.*
> *Let it give your bridges the curve of hips and supple vines.*
>
> *. . . . . . . . . . . . . . . . . . . . . . . . . . . . . . . . . . . . . . . . . . . . . .*
>
> *Just open your eyes to the April rainbow*
> *And your ears, especially your ears, to God*
> *Who in one burst of saxophone laughter*
> *Created heaven and earth in six days,*
> *And on the seventh slept a deep Negro sleep. (87)*

Unlike Senghor, the Caribbean poet Derek Walcott adopts Cullen's strategy of rhetorical questioning as a way to provoke his own confrontation with memory and history. In "A Far Cry from Africa," however, Walcott affirms rather than rejects ancestral imperatives even when they force him to accept an uncomfortably dual racial heritage:

> *I who have cursed*
> *The drunken officer of British rule, how choose*
> *between this Africa and the English tongue I love?*
> *Betray them both, or give back what they give?*
> *How can I face such slaughter and be cool?*
> *How can I turn from Africa and live?[10]*

Duality is also key to Audre Lorde's approach to affirming ancestry through gender and celebrating gender through ancestry. In her collection *The Black Unicorn*, Lorde's remembered women from

Dahomey, Coniagui, and 125th Street achieve voice from the ancestral empowerment of gender; this occurs without Walcott's or Cullen's despair or Senghor's feminization of the past. In "Dahomey" she responds to Walcott's question about language as follows:

> *Bearing two drums on my head I speak*
> *whatever language is needed*
> *to sharpen the knives of my tongue*
> *the snake is aware although sleeping*
> *under my blood*
> *since I am a woman whether or not*
> *you are against me*
> *I will braid my hair*
> *even*
> *in the seasons of rain.*[11]

Rain, for Lorde, is not an occasion for the surrender of ancestry, as it is for Cullen, but rather a moment for control, as when nature presents a challenge to such autonomy as suggested by braiding the hair.

Cullen, Senghor, Walcott, and Lorde represent cardinal points in the way poetry can orient the compass of memory. The differences in their strategies for meeting the imperatives of ancestry and the complexity of their affirmation of self through heritage form the basis of my analysis of the impact of memory and the use of memory by modern black poets. Such acts of recollection give shape to a literature in diaspora whose common racial ancestry cuts across boundaries of language, nationality, and gender.

Memory, whether acquired (through received images as in Cullen) or lived (recalled or recollected images in Senghor and Walcott) or mythologized (as in Lorde), is the poet's chief means of writing the self into the larger history of the race.

## MEMORY AND ME

In my own fiction and poetry I, too, have been haunted by the twin demons of history and memory. My book of poems *Change of Territory* revisits Europe and Africa through living on those charged continents and ruminating on the impact of place on my racial person. The four-part structure of the collection suggests changes in place or sites of recovery from historical dislocation as I experienced them in the American South, Europe, Africa, and during a return home.

In my novel *Trouble the Water* the protagonist is a black historian who forgets the painful aspects of his past only to suffer their sudden and potentially tragic consequences in his family's reconciliation.

Apart from uttering references to Africa or the South, I hope that my lived experiences there furnish the actual phenomena required to call memory into being and transmit the pride of cultural revalidation. My poem remembers the textures of "winter without snow (DaKar, Senegal)":

*Harmattan starts its December howling,*
*hurling grit of the Sahara all around.*
*Don't look to the sky for rescue.*
*Breathe, and you fill up with sand.*

*Run to the woods and the grass has dried.*
*Those baobab trees are the squat arms*
*of grandfathers poking from their graves,*
*some hands waving us out to play, some*
*holding back the brown fog from the blue.*

*It's no trick, no delicate mirage.*
*Screech like a hawk when your feet won't move,*
*nobody hears you, and roaches big as thumbs*

*come crumbing at your toes, the ants to dance.*
*Stay where you are, grow round and down.*

*Remember your father's cough, the hacking phlegm,*
*your uncle's South brown teeth? Ever wonder*
*why fingers crook where they come from?*
*It's your turn to sun burn. Just don't let them*
*catch you combing desert dust from your hair.*

## Notes

1. Unless otherwise noted, all quotations are from Pierre Nora, "Between Memory and History: *Les Lieux de Mémoire,*" *Representations* 26 (Spring 1989): 7–24.

2. Robert Hayden, "Mystery Boy Looks for Kin in Nashville," in *Angle of Ascent, New and Selected Poems* (New York: Liveright, 1975), 38.

3. Ralph Ellison, *Invisible Man* (New York: Vintage, 1952), 260.

4. Ernest Gaines, *The Autobiography of Miss Jane Pittman* (New York: Dial, 1971), viii.

5. Toni Morrison, *Beloved* (New York: Knopf, 1987), 274.

6. Phillis Wheatley, "On being brought from Africa to America," in *The Collected Works of Phillis Wheatley,* ed. John Shields (New York: Oxford University Press, 1988), 18.

7. Countee Cullen, "Heritage," in *Color* (New York: Harper, 1925), 37.

8. Langston Hughes, "The Negro Speaks of Rivers," in *The Weary Blues* (New York: Knopf, 1926), 51.

9. Léopold Sédar Senghor, *The Collected Poetry*, trans. Melvin Dixon (Charlottesville, Va.: University Press of Virginia, 1991), 7. This translation is based upon the French edition of Senghor's poetry published by Editions du Seuil (1964, 1990).

10. Derek Walcott, "A Far Cry from Africa," in *Selected Poems* (New York: Farrar, Straus, 1964), 3–4.

11. Audre Lorde, "Dahomey," in *The Black Unicorn* (New York: W. W. Norton, 1978), 10–11.

# SWINGING SWORDS

*The Literary Legacy of Slavery*

The fabric of tradition in Afro-American literature is woven from slave narratives and Negro spirituals, the earliest and most significant forms of oral and written literature created by blacks during slavery. Not only did the spirituals identify the slave's peculiar syncretistic religion, sharing features of Protestant Christianity and traditional African religions, but they became an almost secretive code for the slave's critique of the plantation system and for his search for freedom in *this* world. Similarly, the narratives identified the slave's autobiographical and communal history as well as his active campaign against the "peculiar institution." Both forms of cultural expression from the slave community create a vision of history, an assessment of the human condition, and a heroic fugitive character unlike any other in American literature.

Critical studies of this material as literature or history have been slow to appreciate its distinctive cultural voice. Marion Starling has argued that slave narratives are of "sub-literary quality" and that their chief importance lies "in their genetic relationship to the popular slave novels of the 1850s," most notably Harriet Beecher Stowe's *Uncle Tom's Cabin*.[1] And historians, until recently, have ignored them as genuine documents because of their subjectivity and possible "inauthenticity."

Further scholarship, such as Charles Nichols's *Many Thousand Gone*, has produced important reconsiderations of the slave community and of the relations between masters and slaves by using slave literature as a primary source. Through the study of black and white autobiographies, folklore, music, religion and art by such historians as John Blassingame, Eugene Genovese, and Lawrence Levine,[2] the black past is now recognized as an active, vital, creative element in American history and literature. Furthermore, we are finding that "slavery was never so complete a system of psychic assault that it prevented slaves from carving out independent cultural forms" that preserve some degree of personal autonomy and a range of positive self-concepts.[3]

Through American slave culture we uncover the roots of the many recurring images and metaphors used to describe the black experience on both a group and individual level. The spirituals and the narratives constitute a literature in that they are deliberate creations of the slaves themselves to express their moral and intellectual universe. These forms of communication, what W. E. B. Du Bois called "the sorrow songs," what Benjamin Mays referred to as "mass" literature, and what Saunders Redding has identified as a "literature of necessity,"[4] remind us that they were created out of the practical need to adjust to the American environment with a burning passion to be free.

Slave narratives were published from 1703 until the first forty years of the twentieth century, when former slaves, interviewed in the Federal Writers' Project, furnished volumes of historical testimony and when men such as Booker T. Washington and George Washington Carver published autobiographies drawn from their childhood experiences during slavery. Published in single volumes both in England and the United States and reaching a height of popularity and commercial success after 1840 when antislavery sentiment was strongest, narratives and autobiographical sketches of slaves appeared in abolitionist newspapers such as Garrison's *Liberator*, the *National Anti-Slavery Standard*, the *Quarterly Anti-Slavery Magazine* in New York, the *National Enquirer* in Philadelphia, and the *Observer* in St. Louis. Narratives also appeared in judicial records, broadsides, and church records. Slave songs were less widely popularized, and no major effort to collect them was made until after the Civil War when William Francis Allen and Lucy McKim Garrison published *Slave Songs of the United States* in 1867.

Both narratives and songs are seminal to the development of Afro-American autobiography, fiction, and poetry. By infusing the dynamic vestiges of an oral tradition and culture into a more formal written literary mode, they create an important slave literature in the United States.

This literature has been called native, naïve, and childlike by critics who wish to limit the songs and narratives to one-dimensional meaning. Granted the "native imagery and emphasis in the spirituals are selected elements that helped the slave adjust to his particular world,"[5] but it is precisely in the slave's pattern of acculturation that the student of black history and culture finds specific ideologies for survival. That Christianity is easily recognizable in the language of the songs and narratives has led many critics to emphasize the spiritual docility and otherworldliness of slave thought. However, a deeper study of the dual aspects of culture contact and acculturation between European and African belief structures reveals that slaves needed a language and a flexible vocabulary more for communication than for belief. Thus it is more realistic to examine how Christianity was "the nearest available, least suspect, and most stimulative system for expressing their concepts of freedom, justice, right and aspiration." In the literature, that Christian imagery becomes "an arsenal of pointed darts, a storehouse of images, a means of making shrewd observations."[6]

Revolutionary sentiments, plans for escape, and insurrection were often couched in the religious imagery which was the slave community's weapon against despair and moral degradation. This literature contained ideas that reached the masses of slaves primarily through the "church" within the slave community, and the men and women preached, testified, and told God all their troubles.

Using the Bible as a storehouse of myth and history that could be appropriated for religious syncretism and a practical philosophy based on historical immediacy, the slave community identified with the children of Israel; but they did not stop there. Slaves knew that deliverance would come, as proven by their African assurance of intimacy and immortality with the Supreme Being, and by the wider implications of the biblical past. Both systems of belief helped the slave know that he could actively participate in deliverance and judgment by joining God's army, singing with a sword in his hand, or walking in Jerusalem just like John. The slave was sure he was experiencing all of history: the past, present, and future. Moses very often came to slaves in the person of Harriet Tubman and other ex-slaves who went back into Egypt, heard the children "yowlin'," and led them to the promised land in the North. Historical immediacy created and sustained through the oral tradition that healing moment of deliverance and salvation:

*O Mary don' you weep don' you moan*
*Pharaoh's army got drownded.*

Upon the rock that was traditional African religion as well as American Christianity, the slave community built a church. Out of religious syncretism and an oral literature they established an active contemporary apocalypse in the realm of their own daily experiences. The historical moment for the slave was never abstract, but imminent.

The time for deliverance and witness was now. The complexity of the religious experience, as well as the complexity of the day-to-day social experience in the slave quarters, centered in a conversion-like initiation, became further testing grounds for individual and corporate faith in the possibility of freedom. And as the slave lived, he would reckon with time, community, and his own life journey. He sang:

> God dat lived in Moses' time
> Is jus' de same today.

Slavery had brought black men and women face to face with the extreme fact of their wretchedness as individuals. Conversion to an inner cult, an in-group morality, provided the very real awareness that individual loneliness and despair could be resolved in group solidarity. The conversion experience emphasized a person's recognition of his own need for deliverance from sin and bondage into a holy alliance with God as the avenging deity:

> My God He is a Man—a Man of War,
> An' de Lawd God is His name.
>
> I'm a soljuh in the Army of thuh Lawd,
>     I'm a soljuh in this Army.
>
> Hold out yo' light you heav'n boun' soldier
>     Let yo' light shine around the world.
>
> We are the people of God.

Conversion also provided for socio-religious mobility and status within the slave community. Conversion also confirmed an African orientation of personal duty on both a ritualistic and humanistic level. Ritual, duty, and creative expression all served as outlets for individual expression without disturbing communal solidarity. Song and personal testimony, as forms of an oral literature, allowed for individual interpretation while they "continually drew [the slave] back into the communal presence and permitted him the comfort of basking in the warmth of the shared assumptions of those around him."[7] Conversion to these shared assumptions provided a basis for self-esteem, new values, and an important defense against degradation. Slaves were initiated through the spiritual potency of personal testimony. They prepared themselves to fight for freedom by becoming morally free of an intrusive and debilitating white out-group and by becoming more responsible to the inner slave community.

Slaves demanded of each other explicit principles of character and right living: for the "soul" to be a "witness for my Lord." This was no mystical yearning, but a real test of character and conviction. As realists, slaves demanded that they be struck dead to sin in order to live again in freedom. In order for this transformation to be real enough to connect with the vital image of deliverance, "conversion had to be in the nature of a stroke of lightning which would enter at the top of their head and emerge from their toes." Slaves, as Paul Radin continues, "had to meet God, be baptized by him in the river of Jordan, personally, and become identified with him."[8]

The status slaves gained as a result was both inward and outward, sometimes manifesting itself in change of behavior from mild submission to active resistance. Here it is necessary to distinguish an important feature of the slave's conversion. Knowing the deep need for community and the deprived sense of belonging for slaves isolated in bondage, and knowing the utter contempt with which whites regarded black spiritual welfare (despite a very false "Christian" religious education), it is obvious that through the religious organization in the slave quarters, the slaves were not converting themselves to God, but *were converting themselves to each other*. As a result, slaves converted God to their new identity and community in the New World and made God active in their struggle for freedom. This syncretic African-Christian God became "a fixed point within and without [the slave] and all that God commanded was unqualified faith and throwing away of doubt,"[9] which was what slaves demanded of each other. Both God and man experienced conversion. Together they struggled for self-expression and the fulfillment of human destiny. "The sins would take care of themselves," Radin has argued, but more importantly a socio-religious mobility has been set in motion, unifying the community. Frederick Douglass himself confirmed, "we were generally a unit, and moved together."[10]

Conversion as rebirth or transformation was a central event in the slave's recorded life. In this way it gave individuals an outline of personal history and made them aware of their part in the larger history of the racial group. In fact, by achieving a personal witness (a personal historical sense or vision in which man is the essential binder of time and space), individual men and women could participate in the larger history and further regenerate themselves by attaining freedom and salvation. Testimonies in the narratives speak directly to this transformation and regeneration:

I was born a slave and lived through some very hard times. If it had not been for *my God*, I don't know what I would have done. Through his mercy I was lifted up. My soul began singing and I was told that I was one of the elected children and that I would live as long as God lives. . . . A building is waiting for me way back in eternal glory and I have no need to fear. He stood me on my feet and told me that I was a sojourner in a weary land. I came from heaven and I am now returning.[11]

And he sang:

*I'm er rollin', I'm er rollin'*
*Through an unfriendly world.*

When slaves came to write their formal autobiographies they emphasized a conversion-like model of personal experience and testimony to construct their own "witness" to the horrors of slavery and the regenerative joy of freedom. The conversion experience helped to organize the individual life and unite it with time and the eternal presence of God. As one slave testified to this historical pattern:

> The soul that trusts in God need never stumble nor fall, because God being all wise and seeing and knowing all things, having looked down through time before time, foresaw every creeping thing and poured out His spirit on the earth. The earth brought forth her fruits in due season. In the very beginning every race and every creature was in the mind of God and we are here, not ahead of time, not behind time, but just on time. It was time that brought us here and time will carry us away.[12]

The use of historical and religious language and symbol is seen most clearly in the escape episode in slave narratives. The nearby woods or the wilderness into which the fugitive escapes becomes the testing ground of his faith in God and in himself:

*If you want to find Jesus, go in de wilderness*
*   Go in de wilderness, go in de wilderness*
*Mournin' brudder, go in de wilderness*
*   To wait upon de Lord.*

The scenes of self-revelation and the experience of grace and a final rebirth become as characteristic to the narratives as they are to the songs. What is developed from this imagery, shared between oral and written modes, is a literature of struggle and fulfillment. The thematic transformation in the text parallels the transformation in its creators. The change is from chattel status, unholiness, and damnation in the hell which was slavery to the integrity of being a man and a saved child of God now walking the paved streets of a heavenly city, the promised North. The slave has been delivered. Conversion was the correlative for a subjective synthesis of history; earning freedom through escape (or insurrection) was heroic action.

That religion and freedom went hand in hand is evidenced by the entire experience of the fugitive slave. Often poorly equipped for long journeys and with few geographic aids, he was alone with only God to help him endure the wilderness. Often leaders of fugitive parties were ministers themselves. One preacher, a Methodist, tried to persuade John Thompson to join his band of runaways. Thompson was unwilling to escape with them, and only several months later did he attempt his escape alone, once he was assured of God's presence. Thompson described the occasion and method of that first fugitive group and his own skepticism:

> The Methodist preacher . . . urged me very strongly to accompany them, saying that he had full confidence in the surety of the promises of God . . . he believed he was able to carry him safely to the land of freedom, and accordingly he was determined to go. Still I was afraid to risk myself on such uncertain promises; I dared not trust an unseen God.
>
> On the night on which they intended to start . . . they knelt in prayer to the great God of Heaven and Earth, invoking Him to guard them . . . and go with them to their journey's end.[13]

Most often the slave's idea of freedom was a consequence of his recognition of his slave status. He needed little outside influence to convince him of the advantages of freedom. Even as far south as Louisiana and in as isolated a region as Bayou Boeuf to which Solomon Northup was kidnapped, the idea of freedom was a regular topic among the slaves, as Northup writes: "They understand the privileges and exemptions that belong to it—that it would bestow upon them the fruits of their own labor, and that it would secure to them the enjoyment of domestic happiness. They do not fail to observe the difference between their own condition and the meanest white man's and to realize the injustice of the laws."[14] Thus, freedom, an essential aspect of human development, was a value within the slave community which also outlined a socio-religious mobility for its attainment. The mobility established in the slave's conversion experience became the philosophical model for further initiation into free status and identity.

The first step in this mobility on the personal level involved a recognition of one's wretchedness as a slave, a realization that one is different and deprived. "I was born a slave," wrote Harriet Jacobs, "but I never knew it till six years of happy childhood had passed away. . . . When I was six years old, my mother died; and then, for the first time, I learned by the talk around me, that I was a slave."[15]

Henry Bibb of Kentucky had a similar rude awakening; "I knew nothing of my condition as a slave. I was living with Mr. White, whose wife had died and left him a widower with one little girl, who was said to be the legitimate owner of my mother and all her children. This girl was also my playmate when we were children." When he was eight or ten years old Bibb discovered that his wages were being spent for the education of his playmate. It was then that he realized his slave labor was profitless for himself. "It was then I first commenced seeing and feeling that I was a wretched slave."[16]

Former slave Thomas Jones began his narrative with the following recognition: "I was born a slave. My recollections of early life are associated with poverty, suffering and shame. I was made to feel in my boyhood's first experience that I was inferior and degraded and that I must pass through life in a dependent and suffering condition."[17]

The Negro spirituals speak to the same sense of wretchedness in slavery as the singers sought deliverance:

*Oh, wretched man that I am;*
*Oh, wretched man that I am;*
*Oh, wretched man that I am,*
*Who will deliver poor me?*

*I am bowed down with a burden of woe;*
*I am bowed down with a burden of woe;*
*I am bowed down with a burden of woe;*
*Who will deliver poor me?*

*My heart's filled with sadness and pain;*
*My heart's filled with sadness and pain;*
*My heart's filled with sadness and pain;*
*Who will deliver poor me?*

The moment of self-discovery has been one of the more dramatic turning points in the personal history of every black American. The moment called for new tactics or behavior that would help the individual come to grips with his feelings of difference and alienation from the society at large. William Du Bois once wrote of his own experience that "Then it dawned upon me with a certain suddenness that I was different from the others; or like, mayhap in heart and life and longing, but shut out from their world by a vast veil. I had therefore no desire to tear down that veil, to creep through; I held all beyond it in common contempt, and lived above it in a region of blue sky and great wandering shadows."[18] That crucial self-discovery, which can happen suddenly and by accident, is nonetheless the beginning of a collective consciousness and group identity. As poet Margaret Walker once wrote in her more contemporary account, it was a bitter hour "when we discovered we / were black and poor and small and different and / nobody cared and nobody / wondered and nobody understood."[19]

By the force of this personal alienation the individual began to see himself as a member of an oppressed group. Within the group experience, perhaps because of it, the individual resolved to remedy the situation for himself and the others who were joined to him by the extreme pressures of racial oppression. The slave could openly rebel or secretly escape. He could also accommodate himself to the subservient role slavery defined for him, as no doubt some slaves did. Whatever action the slave finally took was considered not the end of experience, but the beginning of a long confrontation from which he hoped to wrench his freedom.

Black religion told the slave where to seek liberation: "Jesus call you, go in the wilderness." There a man will be tested, tried, and "be baptized." Religion agitated the slave's search. Preachers like Nat Turner and Denmark Vesey conspired to gain it. Other leaders urged slaves to run away. Turner himself often secreted himself in the woods where he communed with the Spirit and returned with the fresh assurance that his struggle had divine sanction:

> . . . I saw white spirits and black spirits engaged in battle, and the sun was darkened—the thunder rolled in the heaven, and blood flowed in streams—and I heard a voice saying, "Such is your luck, such you are called to see, and let it come rough or smooth, you must surely have it." I now withdrew myself as much as my situation would permit,

from the intercourse of my fellow servants, for the avowed purpose of serving the Spirit more fully—and it appeared to me and reminded me of the things it had already shown me, and that it would then reveal to me the knowledge of the elements. After this revelation in the year of 1825 . . . I sought more than ever to obtain true holiness before the great day of judgment should appear, and then I began to receive the true knowledge of faith.[20]

On the night of his rebellion, Turner met again in the woods with his co-conspirators, where they shared cider and roasted pork as sacraments to their mission.

Other slaves often secreted themselves in the woods, even if only to meditate on their condition. In the wilderness of nature, freedom was revealed as a man's right in the natural harmony of God's created world. Henry Bibb meditated in the woods and wrote: "I thought of the fishes of the water, the fowls of the air, the wild beasts of the forest, all appeared to be free to go where they pleased, and I was an unhappy slave."[21] Nature furnished the slave with examples of freedom and the harmony of all life with God just as his African religious tradition continued to inform him. In the new American environment, the harmony of the natural world was easily given religious significance. Natural imagery was analogous to freedom and revealed a point of contact between man and God. The slave resolved to seek that contact and unity in the wilderness. Frederick Douglass once described this communion: "I was in the wood, buried in its somber gloom and hushed in its solemn silence, hidden from all human eyes, shut in with nature and with nature's God, and absent from all human contrivances. Here was a good place to pray, to pray for help, for deliverance."[22]

From the slave's point of view, the life pilgrimage of man was possible only through a renewed contract with nature, and by so doing he could effect a new covenant with God. This qualification of the life experience is evident in the ordinary day-to-day struggle of the slave in the hot fields and dramatized vividly in the plight of the fugitive. In nature the slave found a guide for the fulfillment of his identity; once he saw himself as a wretched slave, then too, even as he saw himself as a child of God, for the power of God as reflected in the world around him was strong enough to deliver him from slavery. This was one basic element of the slave's belief pattern, and he responded accordingly when Jesus called him into the woods. Thus the slave felt himself converted to the community of believers and to the mission of freedom. In this same wilderness, Henry Bibb stood on the bluff of the Ohio River, perhaps knowing then that in African beliefs, water, as well as the wilderness, was a place of divine power: wells, springs, rivers, and streams.[23] There he meditated and formed his resolution to seek freedom. He wrote:

> Sometimes standing on the Ohio River bluff, looking over on a free State, and as far north as my eyes could see, I have eagerly gazed upon the blue sky of the free North, which at times constrained me to cry out from the depths of my soul, Oh Canada, sweet land of rest—Oh! that I had the wings of a dove, that I might soar away to where there is no slavery; no clanking of chains, no captives, no lacerating of backs, no parting of husbands and wives; and where man ceases to be the property of his fellow man.[24]

In a similar way Douglass resolved to seek freedom. He cried: "O God save me! God deliver me! Let me be free. . . . Only think of it: one hundred miles north, and I am free. . . . It cannot be that I shall live and die a slave. I will take to the water. This very bay shall yet bear me into freedom."[25] For Josiah Henson, freedom in the North was heaven. He resolved: "Once to get away with my wife and children, to some spot where I could feel that they were indeed *mine*—where no grasping master could stand between me and them, as arbiter of their destiny—was a heaven yearned after with insatiable longing."[26] Henry "Box" Brown felt called to escape with the same fervor that he felt called upon to serve God. The revelation also told him how he could escape successfully:

> One day, while I was at work and my thoughts were eagerly feasting upon the idea of freedom, I felt my soul called out to Heaven to breathe a prayer to Almighty God. I prayed fervently that he who seeth in secret and knew the inmost desires of my heart would lend me his aid in bursting my fetters asunder and in restoring me to possession of those rights of which men had robbed me; when suddenly, the idea flashed across my mind of shutting myself *up in a box*, and getting myself conveyed as dry goods to a free state.[27]

The impulse for freedom was very often the beginning of a change in the slave's character. He began to strengthen himself for the difficulties which he would have to endure. Gustavas Vassa, one of the earliest narrators who vividly remembered his African heritage, wrote that in the midst of his thoughts on slavery and freedom his immediate impulse was to look "up with prayers anxiously to God for my liberty; and at the same time [use] every honest means and [do] all that was possible on my part to obtain it."[28]

James W. C. Pennington, the fugitive "blacksmith," had a clear idea of what lay beyond his resolution to be free. He knew that the time had come for him to act: ". . . and then when I considered the difficulties of the way—the reward that would be offered—the human bloodhounds that would be set upon my track—the weariness—the hunger—the gloomy thought of not only losing all one's friends in one day, but of having to seek and make new friends in a strange world. . . . But, as I have said, the hour was come, and the man must act or forever be a slave."[29] The moment of decision and action was sometimes taken in flight from cruel treatment. William Parker once fought his master when the master tried to whip him: "I let go of my hold—bade him goodbye, and ran for the woods. As I went by the field, I beckoned to my brother, who left work and joined me at rapid pace." Parker's escape brought him to the verge of a new era in his life, one that would sustain him over many years because of the very impulse of freedom:

> I was now at the beginning of a new and important era in my life. Although upon the threshold of manhood, I had, until the relation with my master was sundered, only dim perceptions of the responsibilities of a more independent position. I longed to cast off the chains of servitude because they chafed my free spirit, and because I had a notion that my position was founded in injustice. . . . The impulse of freedom lends wings to the feet, buoys up the spirit within, and the fugitive catches glorious glimpses of light through rifts and seams in the accumulated ignorance of his years of oppression. How briskly we traveled on that eventful night and the next day.[30]

The same impulse for freedom was so strong in Henry Bibb that he "learned the art of running away to perfection." He continues: "I made a regular business of it and never gave it up until I had broken the bonds of slavery and landed myself in Canada where I was regarded as a man and not as a thing."[31]

Often the fugitives' only companion was God, and they believed that it was He alone who could deliver man from the death and hell experience of slavery and escape. One recalls John Thompson's reluctance to escape with the Methodist preacher because he doubted an unseen God. But because membership in the community of believers, in God's army, required an unconditional faith in God's power and willingness to deliver his children, Thompson had to be converted. He had to hear God's voice and believe. When saved from a dangerous situation, Thompson began to believe in God's presence and then, started his life pilgrimage toward the salvation and freedom slaves felt was theirs to achieve. Thompson's personal witness united him to his community and to the cause of freedom that he now has the strength and guidance to seek alone:

> I knew it was the hand of God, working in my behalf; it was his voice warning me to escape from the danger towards which I was hastening. Who would not praise such a God? Great is the Lord, and greatly to be praised.
>
> I felt renewed confidence and faith, for I believed that God was in my favor, and now was the time to test the matter. . . . I fell upon my knees, and with hands uplifted to high heaven, related all the late circumstances to the Great King, saying that the whole world was against me without a cause, besought his protection, and solemnly promised to serve him all the days of my life. I received a spiritual answer of approval; a voice like thunder seeming to enter my soul, saying, I am your God and am with you; though the world be against you, I am more than the world; though wicked men hunt you, trust in me, for I am the Rock of your Defense.
>
> Had my pursuers then been near, they must have heard me, for I praised God at the top of my voice. I was determined to take him at his word, and risk the consequences.
>
> I retired to my hiding place in the woods.[32]

Once united with God, man shared in a specific moral code that sanctioned his escape and other tactics to insure success. The ethos of the fugitive was as practical as it was unique. In describing the tactics of Harriet Tubman, Sarah Bradford recognized this aspect of the fugitives' experience as perhaps a consequence of fear during their dangerous plight. "They had a creed of their own," Bradford writes, "and a code of morals which we dare not criticize till we find our own lives and those of our dear ones similarly imperiled."[33] It was this moral code that helped the fugitive identify people along the escape route who could be trusted to help.

William Wells Brown once indicated his indictment of all people as victims of slavery and found most of them unworthy of his trust: "I had long since made up my mind that I would not trust myself in the hands of any man, white or colored. The slave is brought up to look upon every white man as an enemy to him and his race; and twenty-one years in slavery had taught me that there were traitors, even among colored people."[34] The slave on the run was constantly on his guard. John Thompson used his unique "Christian" experience as a criterion for seeking help from others. He was referred to people of *true* Christian character, meaning those who would aid a fugitive. Of one man who offered his aid, Thompson writes: "I knew this man was a Christian, and therefore that it was safe to trust him, which is not true of all, since there are many treacherous colored, as white men." In another instance Thompson inquired, "I asked what I should do; to which he replied he could not tell, but pointing to a house nearby, said 'There lives Mrs. R., a free woman, and one of *God's true children*, who has traveled there many times and can direct you. You can depend upon what she tells you'"[35] (emphasis mine). When suddenly accosted by a party of potentially dangerous white men, Thompson passed among them unharmed and calm. He attributed this to God's grace: ". . . they did not molest us, although they followed us with their eyes, as far as they could see us. This was another Ebeneezer for us to raise, in token of God's deliverance, we knelt and offered up our thanksgiving to God for this great salvation."[36]

Slaves believed that God moved through nature to help the fugitive. Moreover, through nature, God made his presence known by presenting obstacles and avenues for deliverance during the fugitive's journey. Most often the same natural force, such as a wide river, was both obstacle *and* aid. The dual quality of nature in the slave's thought makes it more crucial for man to take an active part in seeking deliverance, for he must be capable of identifying the voice as he did through his conversion experience and those good people who share in God's word: the children of God, the *true* believers. These barriers become an important test of man's faith in the power of God to make possible the freedom and salvation the slave seeks. Again, man must earn his freedom.

When Henry Bibb attempted escape alone, nature was his guide: "I walked with bold courage, trusting in the arm of Omnipotence; guided by the unchangeable North Star by night, and inspired by an elevated thought that I was fleeing from a land of slavery and oppression, bidding farewell to handcuffs, whips, thumbscrews and chains."[37] Once having gained freedom for himself, he returned to rescue his wife and child. Caught again in slave territory, he felt he had to renew his covenant with God; he "passed the night in prayer to our Heavenly Father, asking that He would open to me even the smallest chance for escape."[38]

In the woods following their escape, Bibb and his wife and child encounter nature at its harshest level:

> So we started off with our child that night, and made our way down to Red River swamps among the buzzing insects and wild beasts of the forest. We wandered about in the wilderness for eight or ten days. . . . Our food was parched corn . . . most of the time we were lost. We wanted to cross the Red River but could find no conveyance to cross it. I recollect one day of finding a crooked tree which bent over the river. . . . When we crossed over on the tree . . . we found that we were on an island surrounded by water on either side. We made our

bed that night in a pile of dry leaves. . . . We were much rest-broken, wearied from hunger and travelling through briers, swamps and cane breaks. . . .[39]

Then Bibb encountered the wolves who lived there and who came howling out of the night close to them:

> The wolves kept howling. . . . I thought that the hour of death for us was at hand . . . for there was no way for our escape. My little family were looking up to me for protection, but I could afford them none. . . . *I was offering up my prayers to that God who never forsakes those in the hour of danger who trust in him.* . . . I was surrounded by those wolves. But it seemed to be the will of a merciful providence that our lives should not be destroyed by them. I rushed forth with my bowie knife in hand. . . . I made one desperate charge at them . . . making a loud yell at the top of my voice that caused them to retreat and scatter which was equivalent to a victory on our part. *Our prayers were answered,* and our lives were spared through the night.[40] (Emphasis mine.)

Through prayer Bibb was able to unite himself to the greater force of God and thus renew his own life force. However, his escape with his family had further complications and eventually they were recaptured. Once again Bibb escaped alone and began a new life in free territory without them. This last escape found Bibb secreted aboard a ship which conveyed him out of the waters of slavery and trial and into the promised North: "When the boat struck the mouth of the river Ohio, and I had once more the pleasure of looking on that lovely stream, my heart leaped up for joy at the glorious prospect that I should again be free. Every revolution of the mighty steam-engine seemed to bring me nearer and nearer the 'promised land.'"[41]

Henry Bibb's narrative is characteristic of the many slave autobi-ographies in which the protagonist confronts and is confronted by the challenge of survival and deliverance from the wilderness. Man, here, endures the test of the wilds in order to reap his reward of freedom, which is a direct result of his alliance with God. In the end he will be delivered on foot or aboard a particular conveyance which will provide a secret cover for his rebirth.

The escape episode in nature or secreted aboard a ship is an expe-rience of the womb, the woods, or a dark cover that will give birth to a new man. Escape, then, is the central transforming episode in the death-rebirth cycle of life as viewed by the slave. By dint of his escape and his hiding, man becomes enlightened about his condition and reborn through his confrontation fighting his own fear, the wolves, the deep water of Jordan or the slave "patrollers."

The Reverend Thomas Jones recorded in his narrative that he hid aboard a ship until the time was right, until nature intervened by making the tide flow in his favor, and he gained his free identity:

Here [in the hold of the ship] I was discovered by the Captain. He charged me with being a runaway slave, and said he should send me back by the first opportunity that offered. That day a severe storm came on and for several days we were driven by the gale. I turned to and cooked for the crew. The storm was followed by a calm of several days; and then the wind sprung up again and the Captain made for port at once. . . . While the Captain was in the city . . . I made a raft of loose board as I could get and hastily bound them together, and committing myself to God, I launched forth upon the waves. The shore was about a mile distant; I had the tide in my favor.[42]

In the *Life and Adventure of Robert* . . . the narrator hid in a "cave sur-rounded by a thick hedge of wild briars and hemlock" in Fox Point,

Providence, Rhode Island, when his life in free territory was further complicated by slave catchers. Robert was a slave in Princeton, New Jersey, and engineered his escape by secreting himself aboard a sloop bound for Philadelphia. When his family was threatened and then separated by slave catchers, Robert made a final retreat into the wilderness. He returned to the womb of nature, his cave; as he told his amanuensis, "I felt but little desire to live, as there was nothing then to attach me to this world—and it was at that moment that I formed the determination to retire from it—to become a recluse, and mingle thereafter as little as possible with human society."[43]

Henry "Box" Brown made more poignant use of the death-rebirth theme. He nailed himself up in a box and shipped himself to free territory as cargo. During the long journey he experienced the physical effects of dying: "I felt a cold sweat coming over me which seemed to be a warning that death was about to terminate my earthly miseries; but as I feared even that less than slavery, I resolved to submit to the will of God, and, under the influence of that impression, I lifted up my soul in prayer to God, who alone was able to deliver me. My cry was soon heard."[44] When the box arrived at its destination a friend knocked to see if Brown was still alive inside. Brown's rebirth began: "The joy of the friends was very great. When they heard that I was alive they soon managed to break open the box, and then came my resurrection from the grave of slavery. I rose a free man; but I was too weak, by reason of long confinement in that box, to be able to stand, so I immediately swooned away."[45]

By all accounts the God of the fugitive is a God who offers immediate freedom and deliverance to his chosen people. But this deliverance is on the condition of man's trial—man's willingness to be struck dead and achieve enlightenment through his despair, fear, and solitude. Man with God conquers Egypt and death so that a freeman can be born.

In their long search for freedom, as in their religion and literature, slaves defined life as a pilgrimage. Just as life for the African was a continual practice of maintaining harmony and force within the ontological hierarchy established between man, the ancestors, and natural phenomena, so too was life for the Afro-American a pilgrimage toward renewed contact with God. The slave narrators preserve the dualism between the African and the Christian components in black religious syncretism, and we find through their emphasis on the escape experience that the narrators and bards gave the wilderness confrontation a central place in recounting the progress of their lives. For the narrators, this crucial moment of escape is also symbolic of the fusion of the two divergent cultural modes: the African and the American. Out of this cultural confrontation and, in some cases, moral entanglement the slave is converted and reconverted to himself, his community, his God. By engaging the wilderness the slave, as fugitive, renews his primal covenant with God through nature and becomes a freeman. From this primary connection with spiritual and natural forces, man derives his creativity, his freedom, and his spiritual redemption. His self and soul are strengthened.

In song and narrative, through the unifying image and actual experience of deliverance and survival—a life-affirming ideology—the slaves themselves have defined heroic value as an essential aspect of human character. The journey of the fugitive is but a microcosm of the entire life experience of men in search of freedom, which is also salvation. Samuel Ringgold Ward, himself a fugitive when just a child, has written that men entrusted with such a mission grow with it heroically, and thus the fugitive becomes an exemplar of individual and group ideals:

> The fugitive exercises patience, fortitude, and perseverance, connected with and fed by an ardent and unrestrained and resistless love

of liberty, such as cause men to be admired everywhere . . . the lonely toiling journey; the endurance of the excitement from constant danger; the hearing the yell and howl of the bloodhound, the knowledge of close hot pursuit. . . . All these furnaces of trial as they are, purify and ennoble the man who has to pass through them. . . . All these are inseparable from the ordinary incidents in the northward passage of the fugitive; and when he reaches us, he is, first, what the raw material of nature was; and secondly, what the improving process of flight has made him.[46]

Thus, the life of man that the spirituals and the narratives create for us is one which is grounded in concrete action and one which follows the highest moral persuasions. Man, as conceived within the slave's mythos and ethos, progresses toward spiritual regeneration. Through the test and trial of his faith he has fixed time and space in his quest; he has conquered the future by realizing it now; he has gained free territory by stepping forth from bondage; he has conquered life as a slave by being struck dead. Rebirth and immortality are his rewards. What gave the slave the surety of his life convictions and what made real the possibility of regeneration in this life and a positive, functional immortality in the next, was religion. The slave's religion, indeed his corporate faith that joined one to the other by the example of trial and the witness of death, was a joy and a healing fortune. And the slave has become free by first singing with a sword in his hand.

## Notes

1. Marion Starling, "Me Slave Narrative: Its Place in American Literary History." Unpublished dissertation, New York University, 1946. For a further discussion of the narratives' relation to American literature, see Edward Margolies, "Antebellum Slave Narratives: Their Place in American Literary History," *Studies in Black Literature* 4:3 (Autumn 1973), 1–8.

2. John Blassingame, *The Slave Community* (New York: Oxford, 1972).

3. Lawrence W. Levine, "Slave Songs and Slave Consciousness," in *American Negro Slavery*, 2nd ed., edited by Allen Weinstein and Frank Otto Gatell (New York: Oxford, 1973), 161. See also Sterling Stuckey, "Through the Prism of Folklore: The Black Ethos in Slavery," in the same edition; and Eugene Genovese, *Roll, Jordan, Roll* (New York: Pantheon, 1974).

4. Benjamin Mays, *The Negro's God as Reflected in his Literature* (New York: Atheneum, 1968), 1. J. Saunders Redding, *To Make a Poet Black* (Maryland: McGrath, 1968), 3.

5. G. R. Wilson, "The Religion of the American Negro Slave: His Attitude Toward Life and Death," *Journal of Negro History* VII (January 1923), 43.

6. John Lovell, Jr., "The Social Implications of the Negro Spiritual," in *The Social Implications of Early Negro Music in the United States*, ed. Bernard Katz (New York: Arno Press, 1969), 135. See also Lovell's fuller treatment of the spirituals in *Black Song: The Forge and the Flame* (New York: Macmillan, 1972).

7. Levine, 162–3. See also Lawrence W. Levine, *Black Culture and Black Consciousness* (New York: Oxford, 1977).

8. Fisk University, *God Struck Me Dead* (Nashville: Social Science Institute, Fisk University, 1945), vii. Note particularly Paul Radin's introduction, "Status, Phantasy, and the Christian Dogma." Narratives collected in this edition hereafter cited as Fisk.

9. Ibid., vi. See also Albert Raboteau, *Slave Religion* (New York: Oxford, 1978).

10. Quoted in Blassingame, 210. See also his discussion of group solidarity, 75–76, and George Rawick, *From Sundown to Sunup: The Making of the Black Community* (Westport, Ct.: Greenwood Press, 1972).

11. Fisk, 23.

12. Ibid., 209.

13. John Thompson, *The Life of John Thompson* (1856; rpt. Negro Universities Press, 1968), 76.

14. Solomon Northup, "Twelve Years A Slave," in *Puttin' On Ole Massa*, ed. Gilbert Osofsky (New York: Harper Torchbooks, 1969), 370. This collection contains the narratives of Henry Bibb and William Wells Brown in addition to Northup. Citations of their narratives by last name refer to this edition.

15. Harriet Jacobs, in *Black Men in Chains*, ed. Charles Nichols (New York: Lawrence Hill, 1972), 269. Contains also narrative sketches from William Parker, Henry "Box" Brown, et al. that are cited hereafter by author.

16. Bibb, 64–65.

17. Thomas Jones, *The Experience of Thomas H. Jones* (Boston: Bazin & Chandler, 1862), 5.

18. William E. B. Du Bois, *The Souls of Black Folk* (1903; rpt. New York: New American Library, 1969), 44.

19. Margaret Walker, *For My People* (New Haven: Yale, 1947).

20. Nat Turner, *The Confessions of Nat Turner*, ed. Thomas Gray; rpt. in *Nat Turner's Slave Rebellion*, ed. Herbert Aptheker (New York: Grove Press, 1968), 136.

21. Bibb, 72.

22. Frederick Douglass, *Life and Times of Frederick Douglass* (1881; New York: Bonanza Books, 1962), 135.

23. Geoffrey Parrinder, *Religion in Africa* (Baltimore: Penguin, 1969), 56.

24. Bibb, 72.

25. Douglass, 125.

26. Josiah Henson, *Father Henson's Story of His Own Life* (1858; New York: Corinth Books, 1962), 60–61.

27. Henry "Box" Brown, 194.

28. Gustavas Vassa, *The Interesting Narrative of Olaudah Equiano, or Gustavas Vassa, the African. Written by Himself,* 1791; rpt. in *Great Slave Narratives,* ed. Arna Bontemps (Boston: Beacon Press, 1969), 87. Also contains narratives of James Pennington and William and Ellen Craft.

29. Pennington, 16.

30. William Parker, 290–91.

31. Bibb, 165.

32. Thompson, 80–81.

33. Sarah Bradford, *Harriet—The Moses of Her People* (New York: Lockwood, 1886), 72.

34. William Wells Brown, 216.

35. Thompson, 85–86.

36. Ibid., 87.

37. Bibb, 85.

38. Ibid., 96.

39. Ibid., 125–26.

40. Ibid., 126–28.

41. Ibid., 151.

42. Thomas Jones, 46.

43. Robert Voorhis, *Life and Adventures of Robert, The Hermit of Massachusetts, Who has lived Fourteen Years in a Cave, Secluded from Human Society, Taken from His Own Mouth* (Providence: Henry Trumbull, 1829), n.pag.

44. Henry "Box" Brown, 196.

45. Ibid., 197.

46. Samuel Ringgold Ward, *Autobiography of a Fugitive Negro* (London: Snow, 1865), 165–66. Recent scholarship has expanded the study of the fugitive hero in Afro-American autobiography. See Stephen Butterfield, *Black Autobiography in America* (Amherst: University of Massachusetts Press, 1974); Sidonie Smith, *Where I'm Bound: Patterns of Slavery and Freedom in Black American Autobiography* (Westport, Ct.: Greenwood Press, 1974); and in a broader literary and cultural context, Houston Baker, *Long Black Song: Essays in Afro-American Culture and Literature* (Charlottesville: University of Virginia Press, 1972).

# BLACK THEATER

## The Aesthetics

When we intellectually consider the idea of a black aesthetics, we need not look to Aristotelian academes or white Western artistic qualifiers. We need not be preoccupied with classical dramatic unities or traditional plot and character development. We need not submit ourselves to the arbitrary classes of absurdist, impressionist, surrealist, naturalist, or other available labels which have absorbed new dimensions in American dramaturgy. We need not.

In search of a black aesthetics we need only to look to ourselves. We must probe the depths of the black soul and unleash the wild wings of the black spirit. Its flight will lead us forever onward and upward to a greater aesthetic appreciation of the free black spirit.

The aesthetics of black art come from within. It is the internal made external. For within the creative psyche of the black artist, who must be deep into the reality of his own existence, is born the essence of black aesthetics from its union with community. It is thus the internal consciousness of the black artist from whence come the sole standard, if you will, of his art.

Black artists must not look for absolute external aesthetic criteria for self-expression, for that forced objectivity negates a fundamental aspect of creativity—the *self.* Instead, he must view his art from within the total spirituality of his blackness and create new forms and new standards which offer a truer reflection of himself and his art.

In theater, the thrust of aesthetics is the drama of the black experience. It derives its energy from black life-styles and exerts a positive force toward the dramatic perpetuation of that life. It redefines the theater process into an arena of self-awareness, self-direction, self-criticism in relation to the entire black community. It is a marriage of the self and the community whose child is ART.

As such, black theater fosters a great festival of blackness where new doors are opened, new directions forged, and new aesthetics developed from the "dark continent" of the progressive black being.

It is indeed intellectually satisfying to expound upon the ideologies of a black aesthetics, but the total grasp of such knowledge is missed if the intellectual aesthetics renders itself impotent in practical application. The viability then, of a black aesthetics, or the art of black life, can only be appreciated in the truest sense by its function. It must LIVE! It must live on the streets as well as reside in secluded ivy-covered minds.

The viability, or the living, of a black aesthetics in theater rests in a total liberation from a white or Negro mentality to an artistic awareness of the beauty of black activity. It is functional, active, alive—for a true black aesthetics lives in every black man. It walks, talks, eats, and sleeps with every black man. It is the essence of black existence. It is the SOUL!

A black aesthetics can never function in theater unless there is a conscious "living black." We as black artists in theater must explore every speech pattern, every physical movement, every psychological crisis of a black existence in white America. We must know the indigenous art of black life completely so as to be able to use that uninhibited style as the artistic impetus to a dramatic presentation of the black experience. Otherwise, there can never be a black theater reflective of black life or black people.

We must combine all phases of theater divisions into a communal direction towards the development of an Afro-American theater tradition. Its product is a merger of the black actor, playwright, director, and audience in a common quest for a total liberation to a cultural and political identity, free at last from the rusty chains of Western aesthetics.

The castrated black actor, in what is conveniently referred to today as "American" theater, must regain his artistic masculinity. He must emancipate himself from the auction block of commercial theater and Hollywood glamour. Once free, physically and, most important, mentally, he can then utilize, in a new theater perspective, aspects of black life, e.g. movement, speech, character. The new techniques that are characteristic of black people become one important foundation for the building of a black aesthetics in theater.

The black actor no longer acts or imitates. He lives! He lives blackly. His mind and body are stripped of the façade of Broadway "professionalism" and left naked to discover the mysterious essence of his stark black existence. He is free from current theatrical restrictions to think black and thus give birth to a true black art, which is an essential and a living part of his existence as a black man.

The black actor is liberated from an artistic colonial mentality to that of an independent creator. Once liberated, he serves primarily as a liberator. He is a messenger to the community. He then, in turn, liberates the community to a significant cultural and political awareness essential to the freedom of all black people.[1]

The messenger communicates the message which is the revolutionary philosophy of the playwright. His literature is the prophecy that heralds the creation of a black artistic medium as the only form which fully expresses the aesthetic truth of black life. The playwright is a sculptor who combines various aspects of black life into a soft fertile clay, and molds the spiritual essence of the black experience into a solid living structure, impervious to the intrusion of white exploiters.

The playwright has created, now he must communicate. As a black artist he directs himself to the black community to which he is both educator and student.

As educator, the playwright teaches his people the glory of black heroes, the resolution of social problems, and the art of community politics. He exposes the flaws of black society to foster internal reform. He praises black accomplishments to instill hope and ambition. He proclaims black beauty to show forth pride in being black. He teaches his people about themselves in order that they may appreciate their blackness as a unique blessing. The theater then becomes a great ritual of ethnic identity and ethnic worth.

As student, the black playwright looks to his community as a source of material. He must learn about himself in relation to his people in order to provide a true representation of black life. The playwright learns from the people he chooses to portray. Thus, the black community dictates the technique he must use to effectively relate to that community. Black people as a collective body will dictate the form and content of black drama, and in the end will judge the artistic merit of the playwright as his art speaks for the people and himself. The black community at large is both the source and the critic of the black playwright.

It is clear that the community as a collective society is the center of black aesthetics. In our quest for a functional application of a black aesthetics in theater and the development of an Afro-American theater tradition, we must look first to the black community. Therein lie the souls of black folk. Therein lies the beauty of black life as reflected by black people. Therein lies the black aesthetics.

A functional, viable black aesthetics grows from an alliance of the artist with the community. The artist and his audience become one in search of the spiritual truth of blackness in a righteous effort to create an indigenous black art . . . a living theater . . . a living aesthetics.

## Notes

1. Mr. Dixon wishes to make it clear that this section of his essay (on the "Liberation" of the black actor) "comes from an idea developed by actress Barbara Ann Teer and the National Black Theater, Inc." of which he is a student/member.

Part III

# WRITING
## AFRICAN AMERICAN
## LITERARY CRITICISM

# SINGING A DEEP SONG

*Language as Evidence in the Novels of*
*Gayl Jones*

I

Since the publication of her first novel, *Corregidora* (1975), Gayl
Jones has figured among the best of contemporary Afro-American
writers who have used Black speech as a major aesthetic device in
their works. Jones also holds a prominent place among women writers who have tried to rescue the Black female personality from the
devastation and neglect it has suffered in a racist and sexist society. Like Alice Walker, Toni Morrison, Sherley Williams, Toni Cade
Bambara, and such male writers as Ernest Gaines and Ishmael Reed,
Jones uses the rhythm and structure of spoken language to develop
authentic characters and to establish new possibilities for dramatic
conflict within the text and between readers and the text itself.

Furthering the trend initiated by Langston Hughes and Sterling
Brown, the first poets to explore the many octaves of Afro-American
speech as a figurative language, these writers ground their work in
culture and personality, rather than in ideologies of naturalism and
social protest. They draw their vocabulary from Black music, events
in history, religious symbolism, and the vicissitudes of modern sexual

identity. Rather than merely introducing readers to the culture, they totally immerse us in the racial and sexual idiom.

These authors do not use dialect per se, but an inventiveness of language and a complexity of storytelling. Their contemporary narratives shift among several layers of character perceptions, reality, and time. Where earlier writers such as Douglass, Chesnutt, and Dunbar had more restricted access to modes of literary expression and were primarily engaged in what Robert Stepto has called a "pregeneric quest for freedom and literacy, "[1] today's Black writers male and female are demonstrating their enormous freedom *with* literacy. They transmit Black experiences within an impressive range of emotional and political tones; from despair to celebration, from oppression to liberation, from individual alienation to communal belonging. There is the urgency felt by an entire community to heal a failed suicide in Bambara's *The Salt Eaters*, Milkman Dead's discovery of self and ancestry in Morrison's *Song of Solomon*, and the brutality of sexual abuse and emotional silence in Jones's novels *Corregidora* and *Eva's Man* (1976). Yet each writer also charts a path towards regeneration and recovery. For Bambara, it is Velma Henry's emotional return to the community; for Morrison, Milkman's courageous flight away from the burdens of materialism and dead-weight family; for Jones, the corrective, retributive behavior that halts a generational pattern of sexual abuse and restores human dignity: "The blues calling my name./She is singing a deep song./She is singing a deep song./I am human. "[2]

Redemption for these characters is most likely to occur when the resolution of conflict is forged in the same vocabulary as the tensions which precipitated it. This dual nature of language makes it appear brutally indifferent, for it contains the source and the resolution of conflicts. Yet language is the main evidence writers have to offer in their appeal for justice, human and cosmic. Jones's fictional landscape is the relationship between men and women, a field her characters mine with dishonesty, manipulation, mutual abuse. The battleground is sex, and Jones uses the right sexual vocabulary to strategize the warfare. Results vary; it can be the ambiguous yet healing reconciliation of a blues stanza shared between Mutt and Ursa in *Corregidora*, or a lonely woman's solo cry at orgasm in *Eva's Man*. What Jones is after are the words and deeds that finally break the sexual bondage men and women impose upon each other. When language is drawn from the musical and sexual idiom and shared with the reader like a song or an incantation, there is a chance that painful wounds may be healed. Such reconciliation is possible through an evidence of words spoken, sung, communicated. Acts of language can be regenerative: predatory characters can recover their briefly lost selves by reconnecting to the textures of love and identity articulated in the Black American speech community.

Afro-American language and storytelling tradition are the main sources of Jones's development as a writer. "I used to say that I learned to write by listening to people talk," she told one interviewer. "I still feel that the best of my writing comes from having heard rather than read. . . . My first stories were heard stories—from grown-up people talking."[3] The oral tradition creates an immediate community for the teller and the listener, a situation Jones re-creates in fiction to get inside the story, to bridge the gap between writer and reader, in order to establish mutual recognition and communication. This close relationship preserves and nourishes tradition: "When you tell a story you automatically talk about traditions, but they're never separate from the people, the human implications. You're talking about language, you're talking about politics and morality and economics and culture. . . . You're talking about all your connections as a human being" (*Chant* 353).

The discernible "literary" influences in Jones's fiction come from writers in the orally based cultures of some Native American groups and those of Africa, Europe, and Latin America; from N. Scott Momaday and Amos Tutuola to Chaucer, James Joyce, and Carlos Fuentes. The oral features in the work of these writers make the act of hearing an important element of their craft. "Hearing has to be essential," says Jones. "You have to be able to hear other people's voices and you have to be able to hear your own voice." In her own work, she admits, "I have to bring the written things into the oral *mode* before I can *deal* with them" (*Chant* 354–55).

The distinctive feature in Jones's fiction is not its faithful transcription of ordinary speech but the transformation of that speech into "ritualized dialogue," a form which alters "the rhythm of the talk and the response." Readers encounter at least three levels of linguistic activity: "The language, the rhythm of people talking, and the rhythm *between* the people talking." Language is ritualized in order to convey meaning in the musicality of speech and to explore its capacity to present themes. The quality of language is enriched: "You change the rhythm of the talk and response and you change the rhythm *between* the talk and response. So in ritualized dialogue you do something to the rhythm or you do something to the words. You change the kind of words they would use or the rhythm of those words. But both things take the dialogue out of the naturalistic realm—change its quality" (*Chant* 359). Readers thus find themselves in much the same role of active listener as the writer herself has been. The transformation of oral into written expression (we are in fact *reading* the text) requires a new appreciation of the figurative and ritualistic levels of meaning in speech.

Moreover, spoken language rendered in dialogue or in narration in Jones's fiction allows us to examine character and theme from a different angle: the characters' diction and attitude toward words and deeds facilitates or hinders reconciliation, which is the underlying goal of Jones's characters. Richly drawn and complex, the characters and voices of Ursa Corregidora and Eva Medina Canada offer an evidence of words as their witness to the possibility of justice and redemption through love—a goal that only one of them achieves.

## II

*Corregidore*, in Portuguese, means "judicial magistrate." By changing the gender designation, Jones makes Ursa Corregidor*a* a female judge charged by the women in her family to "correct" (from the Portuguese verb *corrigir*) the historical invisibility they have suffered, "to give evidence" of their abuse, and "to make generations" as a defense against their further annihilation. Ursa's name also comes from the man responsible for much of this pain, the Brazilian coffee planter and whoremaster Corregidora. Ursa must bring justice to bear upon his past exploitation of Blacks as slaves and women as whores and upon his present haunting contamination of her life.

*Corregidora* opens with an act of violence: Mutt Thomas in a jealous rage knocks Ursa, his newly pregnant wife and a blues singer, down a flight of stairs. Hospitalized, Ursa loses her child and womb and can never fulfill the pledge made by the women in her family "to make generations." The novel details Ursa's attempt to free herself from guilt imposed by her physical limitation and from resentment against her now-estranged husband. Mutt, however, is not the only culprit. Ursa learns that she comes from generations of abused women and women abusers. Great-Gram was the slave and concubine of Corregidora. Their child became his mistress and bore another woman, Ursa's mother. When "papers" were burned to deny that slavery ever existed, that these women may not have ever existed, their sole defense is to make generations to preserve the family. As Ursa has been admonished to do from the time she was five: "They didn't want to leave no evidence of what they done—so it couldn't be held against them. And I'm leaving evidence too. And you got to leave evidence . . . we got to have evidence to hold up. That's why they burned all the papers, so there wouldn't be no evidence to hold up against them."⁴ This oral pledge must accomplish what the written record no longer can do.

The pledge not only binds Ursa to procreation, it also revives in her mind the specter of cruel Corregidora himself. When Ursa is abused by Mutt and forced to come to new terms with her femininity, the images of Corregidora and Mutt merge and she feels abused by both simultaneously. Paradoxically, however, Mutt attacked Ursa without knowing she was pregnant. He made it impossible for her to "give evidence" through making generations and she must find another way. Indirectly, Mutt has made it possible for Ursa to free herself from the pattern of *mutual* abuse implicit in the pledge itself. Ursa, haunted by the relationship between Great-Gram and Corregidora, learns that she was about to continue the oppressive matrilineage that held men and women captive to the need for generations in the manner preordained by her foremothers:

> I realized for the first time I had what those women had. I'd always thought I was different. *Their* daughter, but somehow different. Maybe less Corregidora. I don't know. But when I saw that picture, I knew I had it. What my mother and my mother's mother before her had. The mulatto women. Great-Gram was the coffee-bean woman, but the rest of us . . . But I am different now, I was thinking, I have everything they had, except generations. I can't make generations. And even if I still had my womb, even if the first baby had come— what would I have done then? Would I have kept it up? Would I have been like *her*, or *them*? (60)

Mutt's deed forces Ursa to come to new terms, new language, about her personal and generational identity. The different way Ursa comes to offer evidence is by singing the blues in what she suspects is a "new voice" following her convalescence. She is then prepared to confront her past and transcend it as best she can.

At the end of the novel and after a separation of twenty-two years—the narrative's only strain on credibility—Ursa reunites with Mutt. She is no longer a passive victim of abuse nor is she a solo blues singer. When Ursa performs fellatio on Mutt, she retains control over herself and Mutt. Ursa thus exchanges her role as a blues singer whose mouth contains "a hard voice," a voice that "hurts you and makes you still want to listen," into an instrument of direct sexual power: "What is it a woman can do to a man that make him hate her so bad he wont to kill her one minute and keep thinking about her and can't get her out of his mind the next?" The rhetorical question is meant to bridge historical time, to unite Ursa's present coupling with Mutt to the act between Great-Gram and Corregidora. "It had to be sexual," Ursa thinks. "It had to be something sexual that Great-Gram did to Corregidora. . . . In a split second I knew what it was, in a split second of hate and love I knew what it was. . . . A moment of pleasure and excruciating pain at the same time . . . a moment that stops before it breaks the skin: 'I could kill you'" (184). Mutt and Ursa are in the same Drake Hotel where they spent the early days of their marriage. "It wasn't the same room, but the same place. The same feel of the place. I knew what he wanted. I wanted it too. We didn't speak. We got out of our clothes. I got between his knees." The return to their own past simultaneously returns them to the past of the initial tension and conflict between Ursa's ancestors: "It was like I didn't know how much was me and Mutt an how much was Great-Gram and Corregidora." And it is this metaphorical return that allows Ursa to go forward; her reconciliation with Mutt is achieved through sex and a ritualized dialogue that assumes the rhythm, structure, and tone of a blues stanza:

> "I don't want a kind of woman that hurt you," he said.
> "Then you don't want me."
> "I don't want a kind of woman that hurt you."
> "Then you don't want me."
> "I don't want a kind of woman that hurt you."
> "Then you don't want me."

The blues language is evidence for the *re*generation Ursa and Mutt experience: "He shook me till I fell against him crying. 'I don't want a kind of man that'll hurt me neither,' I said. He held me tight" (185).

Furthermore, the six-line call-response pattern above reflects the blues structure of the entire novel and the pattern of Ursa's developing consciousness. The narrative is shaped by the three-part incremental repetition of story line from Great-Gram to Gram, Gram to Mama, Mama to Ursa: "My great-grandmama told my grandmama the part she lived through that my grandmama didn't live through and my grandmama told my mama what they both lived through and my mama told me what they all lived through and we suppose to pass it down like that from generation to generation so we'd never forget. Even though they'd burned everything to play like it didn't never happen" (9). Ursa, however, sings a different song. And like the last line in most blues stanzas, her new words resolve the song's narrative only after she reunites with Mutt.

Corregidora, immortalized by the oral history, is the lover and husband of all the women, including Mama, who, although she married Martin and later separated from him, kept her maiden name. Corregidora also threatens to possess Ursa until Mutt's jealous rage frees her from the grip of those generations. During the years of her estrangement from Mutt, Ursa grows aware of mutual abuse and the danger of her potential acquiescence, "like Mama when she started talking like Great-Gram." The knowledge Ursa gains that leads her from blues solo to the blues duet above concerns the arbitrary exchange of power and the mutual consent which produces authority: "But was what Corregidora had done to *her*, to *them*, any worse than what Mutt had done to me, than what we had done to each other, than what Mama had done to Daddy, or what he had done to her in return, making her walk down the street looking like a whore?" (184). The justice Ursa finally wields comes from the fundamental ambivalence of the blues condition, what Ralph Ellison once defined as an "autobiographical chronicle of personal *catastrophe* expressed *lyrically*" (emphasis mine); from language comes control, a form to contain and transmit experience.

Mutt, although inarticulate about his deepest feelings and love for Ursa, understands her dilemma. His jealousy is understandable on the one hand because he views Corregidora as a rival for Ursa's attention, indeed *love*, and on the other because he feels caught in the abusive stereotype of a male breeder, a role that Martin rejected as soon as he realized the conspiracy of the elder Corregidora women. Mutt was drawn to Ursa by the bewitching power of her songs. Ursa's voice, like that of a Black siren, lures men to a potentially tragic fate. But Ursa is also trapped in the act of luring men. In this regard she bears strong resemblance to Lula in Baraka's *Dutchman*, who never finds her way *out* of the underground subway. Ursa is similarly ensnared by history; she finds release only by learning the truth behind her mother's marriage and by reuniting with Mutt.

Feeling that he knows Ursa "from way back," Mutt is both her opponent and her friend largely because of what he intuits from the evidence of her songs. "When I first saw Mutt I was singing a song about a train tunnel. About this train going in the tunnel, but it didn't seem like they was no end to the tunnel, and nobody knew when the train would get out, and then all of a sudden the tunnel tightened around the train like a fist. Then I sang about this bird woman, whose eyes were deep wells. How she would take a man on a long journey, but never return him" (147). Ursa's attraction to Mutt makes him an audience of one: "he got to be the man I was singing to. I would look at him when I began a song and somehow I would be looking at him when I ended it." Mistaking him for all men, Ursa is slow to appreciate Mutt's individuality or his ability to help her escape the oppressive hold of Corregidora. Ursa is also guilty of trying to make Mutt play Corregidora's role:

> When I'd flared back at him with his own kind of words, he'd say, "You never used to talk like that. How'd you get to talk like that?"
>
> I answered, "I guess you taught me. Corregidora taught Great-Gram to talk the way she did."
>
> "Don't give me hell, Ursa," he said. "You know this is hell. Don't you feel anything? Don't you want me?"
>
> "Yes," I said.
>
> "I want to help you, but I can't help you unless you help me."
> (152–53)

Mutt tries to tell Ursa that she isn't the hard woman she thinks she must be. But she persists in wearing the mask. When he refuses Ursa sex, it is his way of reacting to her use and abuse of him. Mutt's last act of aggression, knocking Ursa accidentally down a flight of stairs, breaks their dual tie to Corregidora—Ursa's womb.

The loss of her womb precipitates Ursa's journey back into the past to recover a female identity that was lost along with her inability to make generations, the main source of identity for her foremothers. Ursa rejects the lesbian advances of Cat Lawson and Jeffey, and has a brief marriage with Tadpole, a bar owner who also tries to help Ursa feel like a woman again. But the only people who can help are her mother and Mutt, who lead Ursa right back to a new kind of struggle with Corregidora.

When Ursa takes the initiative to visit her mother and urges her to talk, she learns how Mama was virtually made into a whore, not by Martin but by Great-Gram and Gram, who needed generations to pursue their rage against Corregidora more than they needed men as stable family partners. "They be telling me," Mama says, "about making generations, but I wasn't looking for no man. I never was looking for no man. I kept thinking back on it, though, and it was like I had to go there, had to go there and sit there and have him watch me like that . . . you know how mens watch you when they wont something" (114). And this is the same look Mutt accuses Ursa of giving other men: "If you wasn't one of them you wouldn't like them mens watching after you." But by the time she met Martin Ursa's mother was already trapped. "Like my body or something knew what it wanted even if I didn't want no man. Cause I knew I wasn't looking for none. But it was like it knew it wanted you, and knew it would have you, and knew you'd be a girl. It was like my whole body knew you'd be a girl" (117). The unnamed force is Corregidora.

Martin's discovery that he was simply a surrogate breeder for Corregidora causes the breakup of the marriage. Martin tells Mama: "Money's not how I helped you. I helped you that night didn't I . . . I lived in that house long enough to know I helped you. How long was it? Almost two years, wasn't it? That's long enough for any man to know if he's helped. How could I have missed. I mean, the first time. The other times were all miss, weren't they, baby? They were all miss, weren't they?" (119). Martin then retaliates by making Mama walk through the town looking like a whore, which is what the other women were, Corregidora's whores. Following Ursa's birth and her divorce, Mama returns to the celibacy she has always preferred. She has fulfilled her pledge and she retains her maiden name, which suggests that Mama is symbolically married to Corregidora not to Martin. Ursa also tries to keep her name in what we must now see ironically as a sign not of independence but of dependence: "That's my name not my husband's." If Ursa is indeed about to repeat her mother's act, then Mutt's harsh reaction appears more perceptive than irrational: "Ain't even took my name. You Corregidora's ain't you. Ain't even took my name. You ain't my woman" (61). Mutt recreates Martin's rage. Martin was not totally defeated by Corregidora or the women because he poses the one question that diminishes the moral superiority these women claimed, for themselves as victims, a question which even Mama was afraid to ask: "How much was hate for Corregidora and how much was love?" (131). Martin, not Mama, had the courage to stand up against the women and demand that they acknowledge their true feelings, that they admit to the ambivalence which governed their lives. Ursa's discovery of this ambivalence both frees her from the past and allows her to return to Mutt.

Like Martin, Mutt unmasks Ursa's hardness, ambivalence, enslavement to Corregidora's history, as well as her lack of identity (although Ursa is on the way to recovering her identity after the visit to Mama). "Forget what they went through," Mutt pleads with Ursa, who answers, "I can't forget. The space between my thighs. A well that never bleeds," and, "I never told you how it was. Always their memories, but never my own" (99–100). Ursa earns her own memory and identity once she hears Mama's story and learns the painful truth that her blues singing, meant to give evidence and witness ("They stuffed Corregidora in me and I sang back in return"), only served to bind her closer to the past. What she must now articulate is not language itself but the rhythm *between* people talking, the emotions communicated in speech, not merely the words: "If you understood me, Mama, you'd see I was trying to explain it, in blues without words, the explanation somewhere behind the words." Ursa tries to replace the ambiguity of language and the pain of violence with a direct exchange of feeling between two parties. That exchange happens in the multiple levels of communication in the altered, ritualized speech between Mutt and Ursa at the novel's close. Ursa has brought memory with her but it is *her* memory, less oppressive and debilitating for the lines are sung by them both:

"I don't want a kind of woman that hurt you."
"Then you don't want me."

Ursa's main task has been to find justice for herself *first*, then the others. Ursa served as nemesis for the women and for Corregidora, as Mutt has been for her. Mutt is also what Albert Murray has called an "antagonistic co-operator"; he helps Ursa break the stranglehold of the past. "Whichever way you look at it," he tells her. "We ain't them." And Mutt rejects the ambivalence cultivated by the women as the family's legacy for Ursa. In a brief tale about his own great-grandfather, who tried to control his anger and bitterness after the sudden loss of his wife by consuming contradictory kinds of food, Mutt offers an alternative: "He wouldn't eat nothing but onions and peppermint. Eat the onions so people wouldn't come around him, and then eat the peppermint so they could. I tried it but it didn't do nothing but make me sick" (183–84). Mutt's lesson to Ursa is that justice is not a blues solo of ambivalence or alienation but a healing communication between reconciled opposites. The voice Ursa gains is the triptych narrative itself, for it returns to Ursa a quality and range of evidence she can sing about and a healthier emotion behind the words she can communicate.

# III

The action in *Eva's Man* begins where the earlier novel left off and envelops us in the despair of one woman's self-inflicted failure to achieve redemption. In fact, the unrelenting violence, emotional silence, and passive disharmony in *Eva's Man* are the undersides of the blues reconciliation and active lovemaking in *Corregidora*. Eva Medina Canada poisons her lover Davis Carter and castrates him with her teeth once he is dead. Important to our brief study here is that Eva never gains control over her voice, her past, or her identity. Instead of wielding language as useful evidence for justice and regeneration as Ursa has done, Eva is defeated by words and brandishes first a pocket knife against Moses Tripp, then uses arsenic and teeth against Davis. Eva never comes to terms with her past; she chooses to embrace received images of women as *femmes fatales*. Ursa and Eva are further separated by their vastly different capacities for love.

In relation to Jones's concern with opening avenues for reconciliation between the sexes and breaking down barriers erected against it from both self and society, it is important to see *Eva's Man* and *Corregidora* as companion texts. Primarily through their attitude toward language and fluency with idioms necessary for personal deliverance, we encounter one woman's fall and another's rise. The clear contrast between them makes Ursa appear as Eva's alter ego and reveals Jones to be a gifted ironist: Eva, surnamed Canada, the promised land for fugitive slaves, contrasts with *Corregidora*, Brazilian slavemaster. Yet it is Ursa who actually frees herself from bondage and Eva who succumbs to it. Eva has imprisoned herself in the debilitating stereotypes of Queen Bee, Medusa, and Eve long before she is locked away for her crime. And Eva remains only dimly aware of her own responsibility in being there.

Other contrasts abound. Where Ursa is the blues *singer* who creates musical language and rhythm as evidence of her regeneration,
Eva is merely a blues *listener*; "I was sitting in this place eating cabbage and sausage, drinking beer and listening to this woman onstage
singing blues."[5] Eva yearns for the reconciliation implicit in a blues
exchange that she remembers from her parents arguing "like they
were working all that blues out of them" (93). One can easily imagine Eva sitting in Happy's Cafe listening to Ursa's hard voice and
substituting it in a negative way for her own. Eva wants to gain the
kind of control over experience that the blues singer seems to possess:
"I wanted to make music, hard, deep, with my breath, my tongue
inside his mouth. I thought of undoing his trousers, making gestures with my tongue, gestures he'd understand, and then his hands
would go into my panties, between my legs and ass" (155). Ursa uses
language more openly and artistically, increasing her awareness of
the metaphorical and moral implications of her songs and the persistent echo of her foremothers' pledge. Eva is inarticulate and brutally
silent throughout most of the novel as if she were rebelling against
language or had just lost her voice completely while filling up on
cabbage and sausage and Davis's penis. Davis makes the connection
between himself and food—"you eat food as if you're making love to
it"—only to suffer the consequences. Eva refuses to talk to anyone,
even when her words would offer evidence in her defense against
knifing Moses Tripp: "I didn't tell anybody. I just let the man tell his
side" (98). Ursa opens up to Tadpole and Mama and, finally, Mutt
in order to have the kind of dialogue with history that can break the
chain of abuse in the matrilineal descent. Eva is shut tight against
her own voice and the advice of her mother and Miss Billie. When
Eva allows herself to be seduced by her cellmate, Elvira Moody, she
passively enjoys the act of cunnilingus ("Tell me when it feels sweet,

Eva. Tell me when it feels sweet, honey."), whereas Ursa brings Mutt within the orbit of her control in the act of fellatio.

Eva remains imprisoned literally and figuratively by her silence that simply increases her passivity and her acceptance of the words and definitions of others. Elvira, more like Tadpole and Mutt in *Corregidora* than the rejected lesbian Cat Lawson, tries to get Eva to talk and, by talking, to assume full responsibility for her acts. Eva's silence is more abusive than protective and inhibits her from developing her own "song" or voice about self and ancestry. Silence also blurs more truth than it reveals and Eva, unlike Ursa with her foremothers, is unable to gain the larger historical consciousness necessary to end individual alienation. Moreover, Eva's guilty silence, her inability to use language, makes her unable to hear others. Eva fails to grasp Miss Billie's important advice about the past and being true "to those people who came before you and those people who came after you." Miss Billie, angered and exasperated by her own daughter's lack of interest in marriage (in making generations), tries to elicit some response from Eva: "You got to be true to your ancestors and you got to be true to those that come after you. How can you be true to those that come after you if there ain't none coming after you?" (85–86). Eva's deafness to this historical responsibility renders her even more deaf and inarticulate about her own redemption. The prison psychiatrist warns: "You're going to have to open up sometime, woman, to somebody." When Eva opens up, she parts her thighs for Elvira, who makes good her threat to make Eva feel something. "You ain't so hard as you think you are. You think cause you can bite off a man's dick, you can't feel nothing. But just you wait. You gon start feeling, honey. You gon start feeling, honey" (45). When she finally talks, Eva confuses fantasy and reality, no longer able to distinguish between them. Ironically, language fails Eva; it has atrophied from disuse. And Eva's sexual coupling with Elvira happens in prison. Eva has failed to free herself or to speak anything more significant than the chilling "Now" at the novel's close which announces her solo orgasm.

Beyond silence, Eva is also defeated by her inability to see Davis for who he is, apart from the other men who have abused. Rather than acknowledging the part she played in abusing men as Ursa has done, which helps her see Mutt more clearly, Eva persists in acting out with Davis the roles of women predators, the images of Eve, Medusa, and Queen Bee which are really created by men out of their own castration anxiety and fears about their repressed femininity. Eva becomes their kind of woman, even to the point of using *their* language: "I was thinking in the language Alonso would use." Ursa only sings about the tunnel closing about the train or the bird woman taking the man away and never returning him; Eva accomplishes the deed, but has no language of her own to tell about it. Ursa learns soon enough that Mutt is *not* Corregidora, that reuniting with him can break the stranglehold of the past. Eva confuses Davis with Alfonso, Moses Tripp, and James Hunn. When she finally decides to share lovemaking with Davis by making "music hard, deep, with my breath," it is too late. She has already poisoned him. Eva's behavior here is demented and pathetic, a travesty of the successful coupling Ursa achieves with Mutt. Davis, fortunately, is protected in death from feeling the effects of Eva's hunger: "I put my hand on his hand. I kissed his hand, his neck. I put my fingers in the space above his eyes, but didn't close them . . . I open his trousers and played with his penis. My mouth, my teeth, my tongue went inside his trousers. I raised blood, slime from cabbage, blood sausage. . . . I spread my legs across his thighs and put his hand on my crotch, stuffed his fingers up in me. I put my whole body over him" (128–29). Eva's active love of Davis in death is proof of her ultimate failure as a woman trapped forever in the limited capacity of her feelings, forever singing solo.

Gayl Jones's primary concern in these novels is with the human capacity for redemption and regeneration. Although the kind of *behavior* seems extreme, the more accurate measure of that capacity exists in the realm of *words*, not deeds. The art of language appears in many forms: it can be spoken communication, listening to grown-up stories and transforming them into written literature for Jones the author; singing, for Ursa the blues artist; or the great abyss of silence for Eva the prisoner who is no more than a murderess.[6] These acts of language and the moral choices they involve can help or hinder regeneration. *Corregidora* and *Eva's Man*, Jones's two early novels in a hopefully long career of an immensely gifted writer, have brilliantly explored the success and failure of the judicial enterprise of language. They allow us to appreciate the craft of language in literature and the healing power of words—evidence perhaps for our own deliverance.

### Notes

1. Robert B. Stepto, *From Behind the Veil: A Study of Afro-American Narrative* (Urbana: University of Illinois Press, 1979).

2. Gayl Jones, "Deep Song," in *Chant of Saints: A Gathering of Afro-American Literature, Art, and Scholarship*, eds. Michael S. Harper and Robert B. Stepto (Urbana: University of Illinois Press, 1979), 376. In the interview with Michael S. Harper in the same volume, Jones makes a direct connection between the poem and the novel: "There is a relationship between 'Deep Song,' which is a blues poem, and *Corregidora*, which is a blues novel" (360).

3. Michal S. Harper, "Gayl Jones: An Interview," in *Chant of Saints*, 352. Further citations appear in the text. See also Roseann P. Bell's interview with Gayl Jones in *Sturdy Black Bridges: Visions of Black Women in Literature*, eds. Roseann P. Bell, Bettye J. Parker, and Beverly Guy-Sheftall (Garden City, N.Y.: Anchor Press/Doubleday, 1979), 282–87.

4. *Corregidora* (New York: Random House, 1975), 14. Further citations appear in the text.

5. *Eva's Man* (New York: Random House, 1976), 5. Further citations appear in the text.

6. The French translation of *Eva's Man* is aptly titled *Meurtrière* and published by Les Femmes in Paris.

# THE TELLER AS FOLK TRICKSTER IN CHESNUTT'S *THE CONJURE WOMAN*

Charles Chesnutt's first novel, *The Conjure Woman*,[1] was published in 1899. At that time white Americans were lamenting the passing of the Old South and creating gross stereotypes of the benevolent planter and his docile child-like slaves.

Chesnutt used these same stereotypes in his novel, which is constructed in a sequence of seven short stories, each of which was published separately in the *Atlantic Monthly* magazine. The stories were later compiled into the present novel structure under the title *The Conjure Woman*. While each tale is independent of the others, together they become a series of verbal contests engaged in by the teller to accomplish many interrelated goals. Chesnutt, by compiling these tales into a single volume, has consciously created a folk novel that describes a series of adventures of equal importance. Thus, there is no single climax or denouement. However, there is a clear progression in the character of the teller, Julius. It is in his character that we find the unity of the novel.

The major plot of *The Conjure Woman* is Julius's retelling of local tales to his new white employer, John, a northerner, who has intruded upon his domain with his ailing wife to begin a grape and wine industry. Julius responds to this threat by tricking this newcomer in order to maintain his residence on the land as well as provide him with steady employment. Thus, the novel describes how Julius fulfills his own material and psychological needs by telling folktales which describe a similar trickery accomplished by conjuring and witchcraft used during slavery.

External to the drama in each tale is the dramatic character of Julius as teller. He becomes a symbolic conjure man as he attempts, through the medium of his folklore, to establish an identity of man and folk artist that slavery tried to suppress.

The attempt of American slavery to reduce black men to the status of children automatically relates the slave's stereotypical character to that of the traditional trickster. This trickster, according to Roger Abrahams's folk study, *Deep Down In the Jungle*, is a child figure who is not "immoral, he is rather, amoral, because he exists in the stage before morality has had a chance to inculcate itself upon his being."[2] During slavery, blacks in America were considered beneath the moral code of white society. Because blacks were considered categorically unequal to whites, the white ruling class was never too seriously concerned with the slave's moral development. Thus, the slave, for all practical purposes, was considered amoral and child-like in the white man's conception of him.

This historical characterization of the black slave is fertile ground for an elevation of the slave in fiction from oppressed man to the dubious stature of folk trickster. In Chesnutt's novel we find, moreover, this character progression on two levels. On the first level Julius is both trickster and teller of the plantation tales. Secondly, there is a trickster characterization in the author himself. Chesnutt as a black writer is writing about a white landowner's retelling of the stories told him and his wife by the former slave Julius. The novelist here enters the psyche of the white listener as he retells the folktales of Julius. Furthermore, Chesnutt himself is aware that he is writing for a

predominately white audience who have a strong nostalgia for the antebellum southern tradition. What the contemporary reader discovers,
then, is a complexity of trickery in the narrative focus of *The Conjure
Woman*. What this paper attempts is a study of the character Julius as
teller and trickster for his small audience, and, on a larger scale, a study
of Chesnutt as teller and trickster for his wider literary audience. Each
person, the fictional trickster and the novelist, constructs an elabo-
rate fictive world which, using the cultural framework outlined by
Abrahams, is a "playground for playing out the aggressions [in which]
he is able to achieve a kind of precarious masculine identity for himself and his group in a basically hostile environment."[3] The identity
struggles on each narrative level are both sexual and artistic.

In the first story the white narrator (I will distinguish Julius's story
from his employer's overall narration by referring to Julius as the
*teller* and his employer as the *narrator* throughout) describes himself as a northern businessman whose only interest is in establishing
a grape culture in the old town of Patesville, North Carolina. He
introduces Uncle Julius as a "venerable-looking colored man" with
"a shrewdness in his eyes." When the narrator informs Julius of his
intention to buy the property and start a grape culture Julius recites
the solemn tale of the "Goophered Grapevine."

The grapevine, it seems, was bewitched by the conjure woman
Aunt Peggy, who "lived doan 'mong' de free niggers on de Wim'l'ton
Road, ed all de darkies fum Rockfish ter Beaver Crik wuz feared
er her" (15). She was commissioned by the owner Mars 'Dugal' to
conjure the vine in order to keep the slaves from stealing the grapes.
One new slave, Henry, who did not know the vine was bewitched,
ate some grapes. But before the conjure caused his death Aunt Peggy
gave him some medicine which made him as seasonally strong and
fertile as the grapevine. Henry's strength and youth would return in

the spring and summer and his old age would return in the fall and winter as the vine itself prospered and withered. This cycle repeated itself for many years. Then one day the tree was poisoned and when it died old Henry died.

The tale seems simple enough when one dissects it from the creative verbal imagination of Julius as teller. But what is more important about the tale characteristically is the process of identification which takes place between the teller and the hero of the story.

We see Julius first through the eyes of the white landowner who spies him sitting on a log near his vineyard. "He held on his knees a hat full of grapes, over which he was smacking his lips with great gusto, and a pile of grapeskins near him indicated that the performance was no new thing" (9). Furthermore, he is described physically as ". . . not entirely black, and this fact, together with the quality of his hair, which was about six inches long and very bushy, except on top of his head, where he was quite bald, suggested a strain of other than negro blood" (9–10). Similarly Henry, the hero of Julius's first tale, loves grapes. He, too, in Julius's description of him, was "er ole nigger, er de color er a gingy-cake, en ball ez a hoss-apple on de top er his head. He wuz peart ole nigger, do, en could do a big day's wuk" (18).

When this new slave appeared on the plantation "he smell de grapes en see de vimes, en atter dahk de fus thing he done wuz ter slip off ter de grapevimes 'dout sayin nuffin ter nobody" (19). The rest of the "Goophered Grapevine" tale is the product of Julius's folkloric imagination; the important point being the character connection between the teller and the hero. This dual character, moreover, this double character accomplishes an important narrative focus as well as a unity of character in the novel. According to Abrahams: "The conflict of the hero must in some way echo the conflict of the narrator and his audience in order for the story to get the approbation of being heard, applauded, and remembered."[4]

The conflict of the folktale between Henry and the master's grape-vine mirrors the present conflict of the teller Julius with his new employer over the territoriality and ownership of the grapevine. That the echo of this conflict is heard and applauded is indicated by the employer's wife's question at the conclusion of the tale. She asks, rather seriously, "Is that story true?" To which Julius replies; "Its des ez true I'm a-settin' here, miss" (33). This point is not to say that the employer's wife understands the story or its implications. It merely suggests a recognition and reception of the tale.

The folktale, however, is not without its moral. This moral becomes the major trick device Julius uses to get what he wants from his employer. The term moral used here may be misleading. It is used to mean the giving of advice in a serious and sometimes condescend-ing way to illustrate a virtue one should live by. In this story Julius advises his new landowner: "En I tell you w'at, marster, I wouldn' 'vise you to buy dis yer ole vimeya'd 'caze de goopher's on it yit, en dey ain' no tellin' w'en it's gwine ter crap out" (33). Nevertheless the landowner acquires the property. He tells us later that he discovered Julius's trick and ulterior motive: "I found when I bought the vineyard, that Uncle Julius had occupied a cabin on the place for many years, and derived a respectable revenue from the product of the neglected grapevines. This doubtless accounted for his advice to me not to buy the vineyard, though whether it inspired the goopher story I am unable to state" (34–35). Here the narrator reveals his knowledge of Julius's trickery which is a point in his favor. But what the reader discovers as the novel progresses are the many levels on which Julius's trickery operates in order to fulfill his immediate material needs as well as his psychologi-cal need for a masculine and artistic self-esteem. Through the medium of the folktale he is able to vent his aggression against the institution of slavery which dehumanized him, and which now continues to emas-culate him in his present relationship with his employer.

As the novel progresses Julius's trick of storytelling assumes gigantic proportions beyond the comprehension of the landowner or his wife. Thus, they are continually tricked, although the white narrator will never admit to being duped in his present retelling of the entire novel as its *persona*. This consistent duping of the employer is the curious way in which Julius assumes power over him and more control over his own life.

Furthermore, Julius, as teller in the oral tradition outlined by Abrahams, is "master of the situation he is narrating; he is the director of the lives of the heroes of the pieces and of the structure in which they are appearing." Julius's storytelling ability represents his "ability to convince and thus illustrate his masculine power."[5]

The assertion of a masculine identity, according to Abrahams, is one of the chief functions of the oral tradition among urban (and, for that matter, rural) blacks who have found themselves in a hostile and often matriarchal environment. In this oral tradition "the sexual power of words is, of course, patent. To recognize this, one need only to see a popular singer or an effective speaker at work and watch the effect of such language upon women."[6]

But the power of the Afro-American oral tradition reaches further back in history to African traditions. Here the spoken word has divine power. Janheinz Jahn, in his important work, *Muntu*, calls this "magic power of the word," *Nommo*.[7] In African tradition, Jahn states, "Through Nommo, the word, man establishes his mastery over things . . . the word itself is force, . . . According to African philosophy, man has by force of his word, dominion over 'things': he can change them, make them work for him, and command them. But to command things with words is to practice magic. And to practice magic is to write poetry."[8] For poetry we might well insert the word folklore. Therefore, in his oral tale Julius gains mastery over his employer by asserting his masculine and artistic power in the verbal dramatization of conflicts endured by his slave ancestors. Julius, then, is "Muntu, man who speaks and through the word conquers the world of things; directs it and uses it to change the world. His word is more powerful the more he speaks in the name of his people, living as well as dead."[9] By the same token Julius achieves a divine power as artist-creator, which his employer recognizes as a certain "air of confidential mystery," in his ability to conjure up images that strike painful truths.

The other tales in *The Conjure Woman*, "Po Sandy," "Mars Jem's Nightmare," "The Gray Wolf's Ha'nt," and "Hot-Foot Hannibal," follow the same structure. Julius is either asked to deliver a tale, or, if the occasion arises in which his needs require that he assert himself over his employer, he volunteers one to mirror his present conflict. In each moral resolution of the tale Julius gains something new. Thus, "any of the battles won, physical or verbal, are won by both the hero and the narrator. Yet he is in so much control of his small universe that he can be both protagonist and antagonist in this contest. He directs this battle as well as winning it. The glory is all his and the triumph is more than just a verbal one."[10]

From the tale of "The Goophered Grapevine" Julius gains a job as coachman for his new landowner. In the second tale of "Po Sandy" Julius gains a new meeting house for his church, the Sandy Run Colored Baptist Church. In "Mars Jem's Nightmare" Julius's friend, once fired, gets rehired by the employer's wife. (She comments: "he was hanging around the place all morning, and looking so down at the mouth, that I told him that if he would try to do better, we would give him one more chance" (102). Following the tale of the "Conjurer's Revenge" another of Julius's friends gets the opportunity to sell the employer an old horse. Half the profit from the sale goes to Julius, who is now seen "in a new suit of clothes, which [the employer] had seen displayed in the window of Mr. Solomon Cohen's store" (131).

The pattern of personal gain is interrupted in the next tale of "Sis Becky's Pickaninny" when Julius *gives* the employer's wife his good luck rabbit's foot. At this point in the novel Julius's trickery, which has heretofore been concerned with survival (the only value traditional tricksters hold sacred), now changes into the more obvious sexual quality that has subtly accompanied his tales and tricks throughout.

What Julius accomplishes in this tale is a subtle seduction of the wife. One will note in the above tales that the material benefits Julius gains at the conclusion of each tale come directly or indirectly from the employer's wife, usually without her husband's knowledge until it is too late to reverse her deed.

This symbolic seduction of the wife by the language and drama of Julius's speech is heightened in the present tale, "Sis Becky's Pickaninny." The story grows out of a discussion of the superstitious value of the rabbit's foot. This rabbit's foot assumes the characteristics of a phallic symbol in the following interchange between narrator and trickster:

> The old man [Julius] did not seem inclined to go away, so I asked him to sit down. I had noticed, as he came up, *that he held some small object in his hand.* When he had taken his seat on the top step, *he kept fingering this object*,—what it was I could not make out.
>
> "What is that you have there, Julius?" I asked with mild curiosity.
>
> "Dis is my rabbit foot, suh." (134, emphasis mine)

The rabbit's foot is no regular foot. As Julius reminds us, "De fo'-foot ain' got no power. It has ter be de hin'-foot, suh, de lef' hin'-foot er a grabeya'd rabbit, kilt by a cross-eyed nigger on a da'k night in de full er de moon" (135). The association of the rabbit's foot with the night and graveyard gives the foot sensual as well as supernatural characteristics. And it is this phallic rabbit's foot that secretly charms the wife.

Julius now tells the tale of "Sis Becky's Pickaninny," which is the story of an implied incestuous relationship between a son and his mother. Their incest is implied by the physical intimacy of their life and the fact that "W'en little Mose growed up . . . He tu'nt out ter be a smart man, en l'arnt de blacksmif trade . . . En bimeby he bought his mammy en sot her free, en den he bought hisse'f, en tuk keer er Sis Becky ez long ez de bofe libbed" (158). The perverse sexual intimacy between Sis Becky and her son mirrors the growing sexual attraction between Julius and his employer's wife. Even the employer, symbolically cuckolded by the masculine power Julius gains through his tale-telling, notices a significant change in his wife's character: "My wife had listened to this story with greater interest than she had manifested in any subject for several days. I had watched her furtively from time to time during the recital, and had observed the play of her countenance. It had expressed in turn sympathy, indignation, pity, and at the end satisfaction" (158).

Chesnutt's word choice here is significant enough to establish a sexual link. John, the employer, then responds to Julius, perhaps out of jealousy; "that is a very ingenious fairy tale." This line indicates a further attempt by the white narrator to subordinate the verbal creativity of the teller as well as his masculinity with the word "fairy" to mean not so much homosexual, but ephemeral and flitty. The wife, however, comes to Julius's defense. "Why John!" said [the wife] severely, "the story bears the stamp of truth, if ever a story did" (159). Days later the symbolically cuckolded husband discovers the instrument that links the sexual flirtation between Julius and his wife: "When I pulled the hankerchief out of her pocket, something else came with it and fell on the floor. I picked up the object and looked at it. It was Julius's rabbit foot" (161).

Julius's trickery has progressed from the level of material gratification to the level of a metaphorical sexual union with the employer's wife. Recall the earlier note from Abrahams on the sexual power of words. Julius's triumph in this tale is a sexual one.

In the next tale, "The Gray Wolf's Ha'nt," we realize the extent to which John has been cuckolded and emasculated by Julius. Here John tries to entertain his wife by reading from his literary tradition in Western philosophy. At once the differences between the Afro-American and Anglo-American oral and literary traditions become obvious from the differences in language, style, and feeling. John's recitation begins: "The difficulty of dealing with transformations so many-sided as those which all existences have undergone, or are undergoing, is such as to make a complete and deductive interpretation almost hopeless" (163). The vocabulary of John's oral tradition, however, renders him impotent. It lacks the sensuality and the vitality of Julius's folk literature. And, more significantly, John has failed to please his wife.

> "John," interrupted my wife, "I wish you would stop reading that nonsense and see who that is coming up the lane."
>
> I closed my book with a sigh. I had never been able to interest my wife in the study of philosophy, even when presented in the simplest and most lucid form. (164)

Julius enters; once again he triumphs. He symbolically seduces the wife with the drama of another folktale.

This story, "The Gray Wolf's Ha'nt," reveals the frustration of the love between the slaves, Dan and Mahaly. The tale's drama mirrors the present dull, frustrating, and impotent relationship between Julius's employers, Annie and John. On a literal level the story functions to dissuade John from clearing the land on which Julius has a beehive that provides him with a monopoly on the honey produced from it. At the end of the tale Julius succeeds in delaying the clearing of the land for a year. However, on a more important figurative level, the story works to remind John and Annie of the sterility and frustration in their own relationship. This implication is made clearer in the last story, "Hot-Foot Hannibal."

This last tale is initiated by a lovers' quarrel between a neighbor, Murchison, and Mabel, a relation of the employer. The story concerns the misunderstanding between two slave lovers Chloe and Hannibal who, by their misjudgment of each other's fidelity, die in separate suicides. From the moral lesson within the tale Mabel reconciles her quarrel with Murchison and they reunite. This grand reconciliation of the sexes in a symbolic epithalamium or wedding festival unifies and consummates the sexual imagery used throughout the novel. The further implication of Mabel and Murchison's reunion is that John and Annie will be reconciled to each other in a more dynamic union than what had previously existed. Julius, nonetheless, will remain the trickster and teller to delight their lives and gain material comfort for himself.

The fact that Chesnutt's *Conjure Woman* was written when the United States was desperately trying to reconstruct itself from the Civil War and the racial polarity that precipitated it, reveals the hostile literary world Chesnutt had to contend with in the social realism of his novel. It was therefore necessary for Chesnutt as a black author to assume the persona of a white northerner in order to mask his real sentiments. In this way Chesnutt's survival as a writer was at stake. And, just as trickster Julius masked his moral lesson in the fictive world of his folklore to get what he wanted, so too did Chesnutt use the fictive medium of the novel to accomplish his professional goals.

According to Abrahams, this fictive process dealing with cultural and racial aggression works best folklorically. "The device of narrative," he writes, "permits free play of hostile actions on a fictitious level; it allows for the construction of a fictive playground in which these important conflicts, which both express and effect the dynamic unity of the group, can be fought."[11] Thus, Chesnutt becomes a trickster in order to communicate his reaction against Reconstruction, the American literary environment, and conventional southern stereotypes through the fictive medium of the novel. Any other means would be prohibited, especially in the *Atlantic Monthly* of the late nineteenth century.

Chesnutt's technique of trickery is the same as Julius's. The author mirrors the problems of race in his contemporary society within the fictive world of Julius and John and Annie, as well as the more distant historical world of Julius's slavery, which for Chesnutt and other black writers of the time was the crux of American racial antagonism. Fiction, as literary technique, makes one way in which that oppression can be tolerable but also creative. In this way the cruelty and bitterness of race relations can be exposed and, perhaps, remedied. This progression from history to fiction marks the beginning of social realism in fiction.

Critic Russell Ames points out that Chesnutt's trickery manifests itself in his seemingly stereotypical characters, who grow beyond their social stereotypes, as the novel itself progresses, into social realism. In Chesnutt's characters, he observes, "there was more than a 'fair' share of well-meaning liberal white southerners, of disreputable Negroes. His method was first to disarm his readers with conventional scenes and seeming stereotypes—for example, with idyllic relations with servants and aristocrats—and then in lightning flashes to reveal the underlying facts of injustice and rebellion."[12]

Thus, as Julius is both folk trickster and tale-teller, so too is Chesnutt a trickster and teller in the larger scope of *The Conjure Woman*. The conjuring effect of the novel attempts a liberation in the audience, and certainly in the lives of the characters themselves, from common stereotypes to real people, each struggling for survival, for reconciliation of the sexes, and reconciliation of the races. Nineteenth-century America would tolerate this message only in the guise of folklore entertainment. But as Julius and Charles Chesnutt remind us through the medium of North Carolina black folklore:

*It's all in de tale, ma'm;*
*. . . it's all in de tale.*

## Notes

1. Charles W. Chesnutt, *The Conjure Woman*, Ann Arbor Paperbacks (Ann Arbor: University of Michigan Press, 1969).

2. Roger D. Abrahams, *Deep Down In the Jungle* (Hatboro, Pennsylvania: Folklore Associates, 1964), 67.

3. Ibid., 63.

4. Ibid., 66.

5. Ibid., 60.

6. Ibid., 46.

7. Janheinz Jahn, *Muntu: The New African Culture* (New York: Grove Press, 1961), 121.

8. Ibid., 132–35.

9. Ibid., 142–43.

10. Abrahams, 61.

11. Ibid., 7.

12. Russell Ames, "Social Realism in Charles W. Chesnutt," *Phylon* 14 (Second Quarter, 1953), 201.

# RICHARD WRIGHT

Native Father and His Long Dream
(*The Unfinished Quest of Richard Wright:*
*A Review Essay*)

*Each day when you see us black folk upon the dusty land of farms or upon*
*the hard pavement of the city streets, you usually take us for granted and you*
*think you know us, but our history is far stranger than you suspect, and we*
*are not what we seem.*

—WRIGHT, *Twelve Million Black Voices*

With these words Richard Wright introduces a two-fold perspective on Black Americans. One is the historical and somewhat ritualistic search for freedom that has led from the rural South to the urban
North, a movement in Wright's own life; and secondly, the mythic
invisibleness of self which this quest has created for Blacks in this
country. In essence, this same doubleness surrounds the most recent
biography of Wright, *The Unfinished Quest of Richard Wright* (New
York: Morrow), by Michel Fabre. However, far from settling for this
existential invisibleness and alienation of Wright, Fabre provides a
detailed examination of the "strangeness" of Wright's personal history
and the growth of his writing to reveal the complex significance of
the writer's journey, his unfinished quest, his long dream.

*The Unfinished Quest* is an absorbing and dedicated analysis of one of Black America's most controversial native sons. Fabre places the writer in the midst of an important personal and historical process. More significantly, Fabre's work is a documentary of Wright's own quest to establish for himself and Black peoples of the world a fundamental humanism which America and Europe had to recognize and one which the Third World could build upon. This was the focus of Wright's personal and political fight throughout his life. Fabre's purpose is "to stress that with his broad point of view [Wright] constantly and sometimes desperately tried as a militant writer to make a synthesis between class and race, between White and Black, between Marxism and Nationalism, between the individual and society." *The Unfinished Quest* is a testament to this legacy of nationalism and commitment Wright left for the many Black writers who continue to follow. The portrait presented here is both that of a rebellious son during the American "hunger" of the thirties and forties, and a stern but dutiful father to a generation of Black writers and intellectuals. Within this development, Fabre finds that Wright "never sought originality for its own sake but rather borrowed what he needed from wherever he found it, in order to gain better control of his reader, to create a new synthesis which bears his original stamp, to deal more blows to his adversaries, to convey his revenge more forcefully and thus 'to build a bridge between men.'"

Fabre, however, is more a social and historical critic than a strictly literary one. Indeed, he finds that although Wright first used literature "as a means of personal survival," he "must not be judged on his writing alone; his career as a militant intellectual must also be put on the scale." The scale measures the shifting emphasis between Wright's writing and his action at certain times in his career. It does not seek balance, but direction, and is socially and historically determinable. Fabre's meticulous research definitively outlines the enormity of Wright's contribution to the social and intellectual history of Black America, America, Europe, and the Third World.

Other critics might say that such a slant does not serve a literary personality as well as his private life and intellectual background. However, one finds that Wright's life is one which is integrated, and necessarily so, with literary *and* political developments. Because of this dynamic combination Wright was able to expand his self-image from that of an American writer to a citizen of the world, a transcontinental champion for human rights. As Fabre explains, this combination justifies a new method: "Literature and politics were two equally indispensable tools in the service of humanism. This is why I insist on judging Wright's work as a whole, not separating his writing from its ideological framework, and not making a split, only artificially justified by his exile, in the unfolding of his career. It is only by respecting this unity in its ideological, racial, and historical context that Wright's importance can be fairly evaluated." Wright's quest, then, is archetypal of a transcendence of political, racial, and artistic identity in the movement from Natchez, Mississippi, to Chicago, to New York, to Paris, and to Africa. Wright's quest leads through a confrontation with the ideologies of Jim Crowism, Communism, Existentialism, and even Pan-Africanism, confirmed for Fabre by Wright's own "refusal to be limited to one definition of himself."

This geographical and political growth is also reflective of a development in Afro-American thinking in the twentieth century. From a writer's point of view it is a confrontation with the techniques of literature and liberation. Wright's life, as presented by Professor Fabre, is the history of one man adapting and growing to realize an ultimate human and artistic expression by personal confrontation wherein consciousness and ideology, the breadth and width thereof, can provide a framework for political and literary commitment to the international struggle of race and revolution. Wright himself admits in *White Man Listen* that "ideology here becomes a means toward social intimacy" (20).

Fabre goes to great lengths to delineate these developments in Wright's activities, his thinking and his writing. And thus we feel the strength and desperate pain of Wright's transcendence. Wright says "in spite of myself, my imagination is constantly leaping ahead and trying to reshape the world I see . . . toward a form in which all men could share my creative restlessness" (*WML* 48). From this quest Wright has given us a body of artistic and philosophical works which provide a sensitive insight into the expanding consciousness of the Black man whose national and international history, whose vision of himself and human society, whose freedom from blood and death *is* fundamental to the rise of modern civilization.

The tension here is double-edged and gives a precision and counterpoint in the rhythm and detail of Fabre's analysis. As biographer and literary critic, Fabre has a two-fold purpose: to examine a man's life and to examine a man's work. Fabre's method explores the work through the social history and literary sources that helped produce it. This approach is validated by Wright himself who wrote, "I and my environment are one, but that oneness has in it, at its very core, an abiding schism" (*WML* 48). As the poet Michael Harper would say, "double-conscious brother in the veil." Fabre's social realist criticism, then, follows the social reality in Wright himself. In this way both Fabre and Wright search through world history and political ideology to find a personal meaning; Wright, the meaning and responsibility of an engaged Black consciousness, Fabre, the assessment of that meaning and the response of the world audience to it.

But for Fabre and Wright there is a further step, for literature has no base in history alone. Rather, it blends with national folklore, mythology, and cultural belief structures to form the philosophical and aesthetic matrix in a work, and fastens character to conflict and control. Fabre is well aware of these dimensions in Wright's litera-ture. He juxtaposes a strictly literary analysis with a very precise bio-graphical, cultural, and political study. What is produced, then, is a counterpoint—the rhythm of a man's life (the essence of biographi-cal research) and the rhythm in the works that life has produced (the thrust of literary criticism). This duality is dynamic and evolutionary in Wright and makes his journey from America to Europe to Africa metaphysical and immediate, metaphorical and concrete.

Furthermore, this doubleness combines the tense, often suspense-ful and desperate search in Wright's personal life with the correspond-ing ideological changes in that life as evinced in the psychological and philosophical thrust of his novels and nonfiction. Fabre's coun-terpoint succeeds in expanding the character of Wright far beyond that of a Black writer of protest fiction or an aloof disenchanted expatriate. Here we find the meat of Wright's quest, an analysis of his long apprenticeship, his maturing and break with Communism, his independence as a writer, and perhaps the most important native *father* to modern Black writers. Here Wright becomes symbolic of the type of literary and nationalistic vision we are practicing today.

Such an approach to Wright is no easy task as the six-hundred-odd pages of Fabre's text indicate. And Fabre must be commended for revealing through these pages the contrast and juxtaposition of Wright's personal life with his public political and literary life, the long ordeal of an American who dared criticize his country "as an American," moreso as "a Western man of color." From that vantage point Wright forges a humanism essential to both literature and liberation.

The final vision of *The Unfinished Quest* is one of hope and con-tinuity. We learn from Fabre's discussions of Wright's unpublished manuscripts just where he was headed at the time of his unexpected death in 1960. As readers must consider Wright's life and work as unfinished, and, taking Fabre's title as seriously as he wants us to, we can look more carefully at Wright's later works from a biographical point of view.

From this perspective Wright's last published novel, *The Long Dream*, can suggest his return to the States in the guise of his protagonist in Mississippi, and historically, in Wright's own attempt to establish a link with America, Europe, and Africa from a Black Western position. This slant shows that Wright was not altogether estranged from an American context, and that he could use this American context as a stepping stone into the more crucial arena of world racism. Thus, out of this creative response to the condition of the Third World, Wright could establish a literary reference for Pan-Africanism as his earlier work, *White Man Listen*, established on a theoretical plane.

Wright's quest *is* unfinished, his long dream still reaching toward a clarity of character and action. Accepting Fabre's discussion of Wright's unpublished "Island of Hallucinations," we are forced to view Wright not only as the vivid realist author of *Black Boy* and *Native Son*, but also of a *series of works*, philosophical and sometimes poetic, which define a new consciousness to challenge America, Europe, and Africa herself for a new view of man, a man driven to forge his humanity from the history of world oppression in order to establish an empire for Freedom and Unity.

Wright's quest also reveals itself thematically. Of special note is the change of emphasis in the family relationship between the mother and son in both *Black Boy* and *Native Son* to the more psychological and mythic relationship between the father and son in *The Long Dream*: Both works are concerned with an initiation into manhood, but in *The Long Dream* we find a masculine definition of the world. This, for Wright, is a new quality of vision. It is the same battle but fought with different artillery; the psychological which manifests itself in the realm of dreams. It is the dream which ties both Tyree and Fishbelly to America, but it is the dream which finally saves Fishbelly.

In *The Long Dream* Fishbelly is advised by his father: "A Black man's a dream son, a dream that can't come true. Dream, Fish. But be careful what you dream. Dream only what can happen. If you ever find yourself dreaming something that can't happen, then choke it back, 'cause there's too many that can't come true. Don't force your dreams, son; if you do, you'll die, you'll be just one more black man dead" (73). The advice here is practical and direct. Through Tyree's premonitions of his own death he offers Fishbelly this definition of dreams, of quests, and even of realities. Fishbelly pursues some form of his dream and tries to create a new life for himself away from the death business in America. Wright, by focusing on Fishbelly's decision to leave the South and America for his own survival, is, in effect, reconsidering his own reasons for leaving America and following his own long dream. Where that dream led was to another testing ground with a few new rules for the same fight.

The final lines of *The Long Dream* provide a poetic assessment of this viable, practical (non-deferrable) dream. Fishbelly "prayed wordlessly that a bright, bursting tyrant of living sun would soon lay down its golden laws to loosen the locked legions of his heart and cast the shadow of his dream athwart the stretches of time."

What follows is a new adventure for Fishbelly as it did for Wright himself. As Fabre points out, Wright's unpublished *Islands of Hallucinations* continued with Fishbelly in Paris and then in Algeria and back to the States, completing what might have become an heroic cycle, a mythic "eternal" return. This movement, in essence, is Wright's unfinished business in establishing a political, cultural, and literary context for the birth of the Black man of the *world*. This new redeemer, born of world conflict and now the healer to it, becomes the father to generations of dreamers, visionaries, poets who will not be deferred. Wright's own growing convictions expressed in *White Man Listen* confirm this trend in his thinking: "I am convinced that the humble, fragile dignity of man, buttressed by a tough-souled pragmatism, implemented by methods of trial and error, can sufficiently sustain and nourish human life, can endow it with ample and durable meaning. . . . I believe that art has its own autonomy, a self-sufficiency that extends beyond, and independent of, the spheres of political and priestly power or sanction" (50).

Finally, Wright's journey as presented in his own writing and in Fabre's *The Unfinished Quest* helps us to understand the international audience and voice of the Black American writer. It also helps us reconsider the relationship between literature and liberation. The Black writer's cultural tools are many, and diverse ideologies, dreams, and responsibilities can build, transcontinentally, a "bridge between men." From both Wright and Fabre we understand how crucial Freedom is as an international question and one to which the universal dimension of Wright's work continued to speak. Wright's literature and liberation are born of this struggle and worked to defend his humanity and vision, his voice and dream through the tool of language, the politics of direct cultural confrontation, the aesthetics of myth and world history, to become a living quest, unfinished, but not undone, and clearly, not "just one more black dream dead."

Part IV

# WRITING
## AT THE END

# I'LL BE SOMWHERE
# LISTENING FOR MY NAME

## PART 1: IN THE FAMILY

*When He calls me, I will answer*
*When He calls me, I will answer*
*When He calls me, I will answer*
*I'll be somewhere listening for my name*
*I'll be somewhere listening*

As gay men and lesbians, we are the sexual niggers of our society. Some of you may have never before been treated like a second class, disposable citizen. Some of you have felt a certain privilege and protection in being white, which is not to say that others are accustomed to or have accepted being racial niggers, and feel less alienated. Since I have never encountered a person of no color, I assume that we are all persons of color. Like fashion victims, though, we are led to believe that some colors are more acceptable than others, and those acceptable colors have been so endowed with universality and desirability that the color hardly seems to exist at all—except, of course, to those who are of a different color and pushed outside the rainbow. My own fantasy is to be locked inside a Benetton ad.

No one dares call us sexual niggers, at least not to our faces. But the epithets can be devastating or entertaining: We are faggots and dykes, sissies and bulldaggers. We are funny, sensitive, Miss Thing, friends of Dorothy, or men with "a little sugar in the blood," and we call ourselves what we will. As an anthropologist/linguist friend of mine calls me in one breath, "Miss Lady Sister Woman Honey Girl Child."

Within this environment of sexual and racial niggerdom, recovery isn't easy. Sometimes it is like trying to fit a size 12 basketball player's foot into one of Imelda Marcos's pumps. The color might be right, but the shoe still pinches. Or, for the more fashionable lesbians in the audience, lacing up those combat boots only to have extra eyelets staring you in the face, and you feel like Olive Oyl gone trucking after Minnie Mouse.

As for me, I've become an acronym queen: BGM ISO same or other. HIV plus or minus. CMV, PCP, MAI, AZT, ddI, ddC. Your prescription gets mine.

Remember those great nocturnal emissions of your adolescent years? They told us we were men, and the gooey stuff proved it. Now in the 1990s, our nocturnal emissions are night sweats, inspiring fear, telling us we are mortal and sick, and that time is running out.

In my former neighborhood in Manhattan, I was a member of the 4H Club: the Happy Homosexuals of Hamilton Heights. Now it is the 3D Club: the dead, the dying, those in despair. I used to be in despair; now I'm just dying.

I come to you bearing witness to a broken heart; I come to you bearing witness to a broken body—but a witness to an unbroken spirit. Perhaps it is only to you that such witness can be brought and its jagged edges softened a bit and made meaningful. We are facing the loss of our entire generation. Lesbians lost to various cancers, gay men lost to AIDS. What kind of witness will You bear? What truth-telling are you brave enough to utter and endure the consequences of your unpopular message?

Last summer my lover Richard died. We had been lovers for twelve years. His illness and death were so much a part of my illness and life that I felt that I, too, had died. I'm just back from Florida, visiting his family and attending the unveiling of his headstone. Later this month, our attorney will file the necessary papers for the settling of Richard's estate, and I shall return to our summer home in Provincetown without him, but not without the rich memories of our many years there. And he is everywhere inside me listening for his name.

I've lost Richard, I've lost vision in one eye, I've lost the contact of people I thought were friends, I've lost the future tense from my vocabulary, I've lost my libido, and I've lost more weight and appetite than Nutri-System would want to claim.

My life is closing. Oh, I know all the clichés: "We all have to die" and "Everything comes to an end." But when is an ending a closure and when does closure become a new beginning? Not always. It is not automatic. We have to work at it. If an end is termination, closure involves the will to remember, which gives new life to memory.

As creators, we appear to strike a bargain with the immortality we assume to be inherent in art. Our work exists outside us and will have a life independent of us. Doris Grumbach, in her recent book *Coming into the End Zone*, reminds us of the life of books: "Let the book make its own way, even through the thick forest of competitors, compelling readers by the force of its words and its vision."

I am reminded of a poignant line from George Whitmore, who struck a Faustian bargain with AIDS: If he wrote about it, perhaps he wouldn't get it. George, as you know, lost that battle, but his books are still with us. His two novels are *The Confessions of Danny Slocum* and *Nebraska*. His harrowing reporting on AIDS is called *Someone Was Here*. And now George is somewhere listening for his name, hearing it among us.

I am not above bargaining for time and health. And I am troubled by the power of prophecy inherent in art. One becomes afraid to write because one's wildest speculations may in fact come true. I wrote all the AIDS poems published in Michael Klein's *Poets for Life* before I knew I was HIV-positive. I was responding in part to my sense of isolation and helplessness as friends of mine fell ill. And when I published the poem "And These Are Just a Few" in the *Kenyon Review*, I made a point of acknowledging the dead and those yet fighting for life. I'm sorry to report that of the twenty people mentioned in the poem, only two are presently alive.

As writers, we are a curious lot. We begin our projects with much apprehension about the blank page. But then as the material assumes its life, we resist writing that last stanza or paragraph. We want to avoid putting a final period to it all. Readers are no better. We all want to know what new adventures await Huck Finn or if Ishmael finally "comes out" following his "marriage" with Queequeg. As sequels go, I'm not sure the world needed Ripley's extension to *Gone with the Wind*, but consider *Rocky 10*, in which the son of the erstwhile fighter discovers he is gay and must take on the arch villain Harry Homophobia. Would the title have to be changed to *Rockette?*

Then there is the chilling threat of erasure.

Gregory, a friend and former student of mine, died last fall. On the day following a memorial service for him, we all were having lunch and laughing over our fond memories of Greg and his many accomplishments as a journalist. Suddenly his lover had a shock. He had forgotten the remaining copies of the memorial program in the rental car he had just returned. Frantic to retrieve the programs, which had Greg's picture on the cover and reprints of his autobiographical essays inside, his lover called the rental agency to reclaim the material. They had already cleaned the car, but he could come out there, they said, and dig through the dumpster for whatever he could find. Hours later, the lover returned empty-handed, the paper programs already shredded, burned, and the refuse carted away. Greg had been cremated once again, but this time without remains or a classy urn to house them. The image of Greg's lover sifting through the dumpster is more haunting than the reality of Greg's death, for Greg had made his peace with the world. The world, however, had not made its peace with him.

His siblings refused to be named in one very prominent obituary, and Greg's gayness and death from AIDS were not to be mentioned at the memorial service. Fortunately, few of us heeded the family's prohibition. While his family and society may have wanted to dispose of Greg even after his death, some of us tried to reclaim him and love him again and only then release him.

I was reminded of how vulnerable we are as gay men, as black gay men, to the disposal or erasure of our lives.

But Greg was a writer, a journalist who had written on AIDS, on the business world, and on his own curious life journey from his birth in the poor Anacostia district of Washington, D.C., to scholarships that allowed him to attend Exeter and then Williams College and on to the city desks of our nation's most prominent newspapers. His words are still with us, even if his body and those gorgeous programs are gone. And Greg is somewhere listening for his name.

We must, however, guard against the erasure of our experience and our lives. As white gays become more and more prominent—and acceptable to mainstream society—they project a racially exclusive image of gay reality. Few men of color will ever be found on the covers of the *Advocate* or *New York Native*. As white gays deny multiculturalism among gays, so too do black communities deny multisexualism among its members. Against this double cremation, we must leave the legacy of our writing and our perspectives on gay and straight experiences.

Our voice is our weapon.

Several months ago the editors of *Lambda Book Report* solicited comments from several of us about the future of gay and lesbian publishing. My comments began by acknowledging my grief for writers who had died before they could make a significant contribution to the literature. The editors said my comments suggested a "bleak and nonexistent future" for gay publishing. Although I still find it difficult to imagine a glorious future for gay publishing, that does not mean I cannot offer some concrete suggestion to ensure that a future does exist.

First, reaffirm the importance of cultural diversity in our community. Second, preserve our literary heritage by posthumous publications and reprints, and third, establish grants and fellowships to ensure that our literary history is written and passed on to others. I don't think these comments are bleak, but they should remind us of one thing: We alone are responsible for the preservation and future of our literature.

If we don't buy our books, they won't get published. If we don't talk about our books, they won't get reviewed. If we don't write our books, they won't get written.

As for me, I may not be well enough or alive next year to attend the lesbian and gay writers conference, but I'll be somewhere listening for my name.

I may not be around to celebrate with you the publication of gay literary history. But I'll be somewhere listening for my name.

If I don't make it to Tea Dance in Provincetown or the Pines, I'll be somewhere listening for my name.

You, then, are charged by the possibility of your good health, by the broadness of your vision, to remember us.

# INDEX